Grammar 1
Clear and Simple

John R. Boyd • Mary Ann Boyd

McGraw-Hill Contemporary

Acknowledgments

Our thanks to

Erik Gundersen, for his insights and advice in the formation and execution of this project,

Tina Carver, for her support and confidence throughout the process,

Louis Carrillo, for his dedication to perfection, which was a constant inspiration to us in the writing of this series.

And our love and thanks to

Sarah and Aaron, Justin and Heather, Anna and Allison, for their unwavering love and support.

—J.B. and M.A.B.

Grammar Clear and Simple 1, 1st edition

Published by McGraw-Hill/Contemporary, a business unit of The McGraw-Hill Companies, Inc., 1221 Avenue of the Americas, New York, NY 10020. Copyright © 2003 by The McGraw-Hill Companies, Inc. All rights reserved. No part of this publication may be reproduced or distributed in any form or by any means, or stored in a database or retrieval system, without the prior written consent of The McGraw-Hill Companies, Inc., including, but not limited to, in any network or other electronic storage or transmission, or broadcast for distance learning.

This book is printed on recycled, acid-free paper containing 10% postconsumer waste.

6 7 8 9 10 QPD 08 07

ISBN-13: 978-0-07-282068-3 (Domestic Version)
ISBN-10: 0-07-282068-3
ISBN-13: 978-0-07-121883-2 (International Version)
ISBN-10: 0-07-121883-1

Editorial director: *Tina B. Carver*
Senior managing editor: *Erik Gundersen*
Developmental editor: *Louis Carrillo*
Director of North American marketing: *Thomas P. Dare*
Cover and interior illustrations: *Eldon Doty*
Interior design: *Design 5 Creatives*
Production: *Genevieve Kelley, Raven Bongiani, A Good Thing, Inc.*
Printer: *Quebecor World*

www.mhcontemporary.com

McGraw-Hill Contemporary

To the Teacher

"Our beginning-level students have profoundly influenced our approach to teaching. We are continuously renewed by these students, who come to us with their unique needs and desire for security and success. *Grammar Clear and Simple* is for them."

–John and Mary Ann Boyd

For over 25 years John and Mary Ann Boyd taught in the Illinois State University Laboratory Schools while also teaching in summer programs at Harvard University and Saint Michael's College. They have taught in Fiji, Japan, and China and conducted teacher education workshops throughout the United States and in the Philippines and Thailand. The Boyds have written several English-as-a-second/foreign-language texts, specializing in materials for beginning learners. Both John and Mary Ann are past presidents of Illinois TESOL/BE. In 2003 Mary Ann was elected to a three-year term on the Board of Directors of International TESOL.

Grammar Clear and Simple is a two-book series for beginning English language students that engages them in meaningful language practice. Book 1 gradually and gently introduces beginning students to the basic elements of English. Book 2 builds on that foundation and brings students to a deeper and richer understanding of basic English grammar.

Each of the 12 chapters is organized into a carefully sequenced set of activities that guides students from **receptive awareness** to **meaningful production**. Every chapter presents a core a set of basic grammatical structures. Each structure (with its associated vocabulary) is the focus of one lesson. This format allows teachers to present, practice, and reinforce the target structure in a single class session.

The first activity in each chapter introduces controlled vocabulary through pictures. The second activity checks students' comprehension. It is followed by a spelling dictation of the new vocabulary. Subsequent activities integrate the new vocabulary into a **strong contextual framework**. This strong contextual framework promotes successful language acquisition through speaking, reading, and writing exercises and group work. Dialogs and narrative passages provide students with opportunities to hear and internalize the natural flow of English. The innovative and effective caret passages (the students must listen closely to the passage to find the points at which words are missing) focus students' attention on new structures in a gamelike format. Word searches improve students' retention of vocabulary and strengthen students' spelling skills.

Notes to the teacher and a tapescript of all listening activities appear in the "Back of the Book." A separate Answer Key for Books 1 and 2 contains exercise answers and midterm and final tests.

Through the activities of *Grammar Clear and Simple* students will learn basic English vocabulary, and will, at the same time, internalize the grammar underlying basic English. With this text the task of learning English is not difficult and complex; rather, it is **clear and simple.**

Contents

vi	Overview			
2	**The Basics**			
	2	Lesson 1	numbers 1-10	zero telephone numbers
	4	Lesson 2	alphabet	
6	**Chapter 1**	**To be**		
	6	Lesson 1	there is, there are is there?, are there?	days of the week names
	8	Lesson 2	it is, they are singular/plural	countries cities
	12	Lesson 3	subject pronouns with *to be* contractions and negatives with *to be* questions with *to be*	nationalities
	16	Lesson 4	questions with *to be* short answers with *to be*	
20	**Chapter 2**	**Prepositions**		
	20	Lesson 1	prepositions of place	classroom objects
	24	Lesson 2	prepositions of place possessive adjectives Who is?	parts of the head
	28	Lesson 3	before, after, between What is?, What are?	numbers 10-20 numbers 10-100
	32	Lesson 4	prepositions of place Where is?, Where are?	
36	**Chapter 3**	**To have**		
	36	Lesson 1	have, has *do* and *does* with *have*	family terms
	40	Lesson 2	do not, does not	parts of the body
	44	Lesson 3	possessive adjectives	
	48	Lesson 4	Who is?, Who are?	
52	**Chapter 4**	**Present tenses** **going-to future**		
	52	Lesson 1	simple present	direction words action verbs
	56	Lesson 2	simple present adjectives all/some/any	
	60	Lesson 3	present continuous or, but	clothing colors
	64	Lesson 4	*going-to* future	sports

68	**Chapter 5**	**Future with *will***	
	68	Lesson 1	*will*	times
	72	Lesson 2	ordinal numbers *comes before/follows*	months of the year holidays
	76	Lesson 3	*will not, won't*	birthday, age

80	**Chapter 6**	**Review**

84	**Chapter 7**	***Can, cannot, can't*** ***know how to*** ***be able to***	
	84	Lesson 1	*can, cannot*	parts of the body animals
	88	Lesson 2	*can, can't* *know how to*	musical instruments games
	92	Lesson 3	*be able to* *because*	sports equipment

96	**Chapter 8**	***Was, were*** ***had*** ***did***	
	96	Lesson 1	*was, were*	shapes
	99	Lesson 2	*was, wasn't* *had*	community places
	104	Lesson 3	*did, didn't*	

108	**Chapter 9**	**Simple past** **adjectives**	
	108	Lesson 1	simple past	weather adjectives
	112	Lesson 2	simple past affirmative and negative	weather words
	116	Lesson 3	adjectives	seasons opposites

120	**Chapter 10**	**Comparatives**	
	120	Lesson 1	*larger, smaller*	numbers above 100 oceans, continents
	124	Lesson 2	*-er* adjectives with *than* *the same as*	money
	128	Lesson 3	*more/less than* *more/fewer than*	measurement terms city populations

132	**Chapter 11**	**Objects, object pronouns**	
	132	Lesson 1	object pronouns	
	136	Lesson 2	objects	
	140	Lesson 3	object pronouns *get*	stores

144	**Chapter 12**	**Summary**	**146**

148	**Back of the Book: instructions, tapescripts**

170	**Index**

Overview

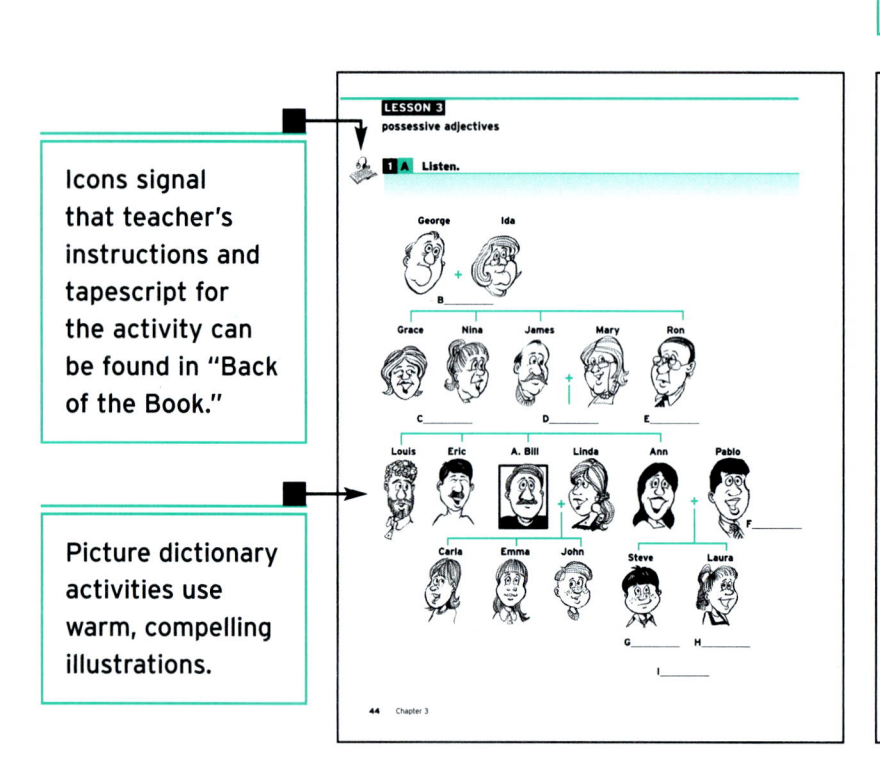

Key grammatical elements are highlighted with clear and simple explanations.

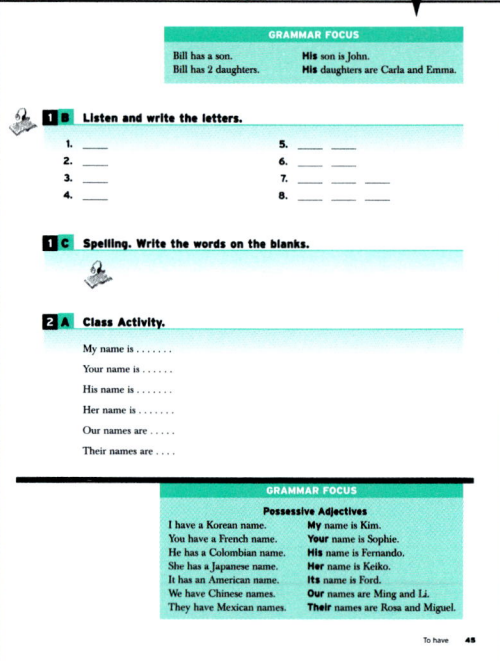

Icons signal that teacher's instructions and tapescript for the activity can be found in "Back of the Book."

Picture dictionary activities use warm, compelling illustrations.

Game activities reinforce vocabulary, spelling, and alphabetizing.

Students interact with each other. Partner activities personalize new structures and vocabulary.

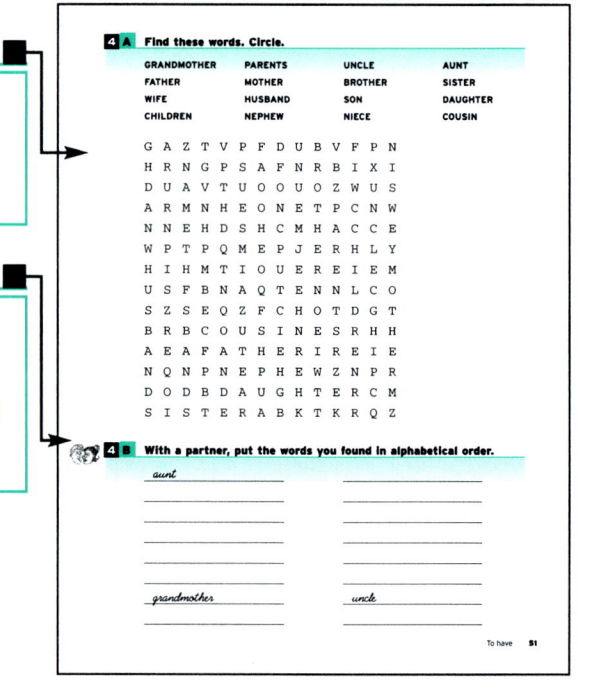

- Vocabulary is introduced through pictures.
- Matching activities check comprehension.
- Strong contextual meaning is central to reading and writing activities.
- Class activities create a context for meaningful practice.
- Spelling activities reinforce new vocabulary.
- Dialogs and narratives focus students' attention on the flow of English. Students first identify where words are missing, then write in words.

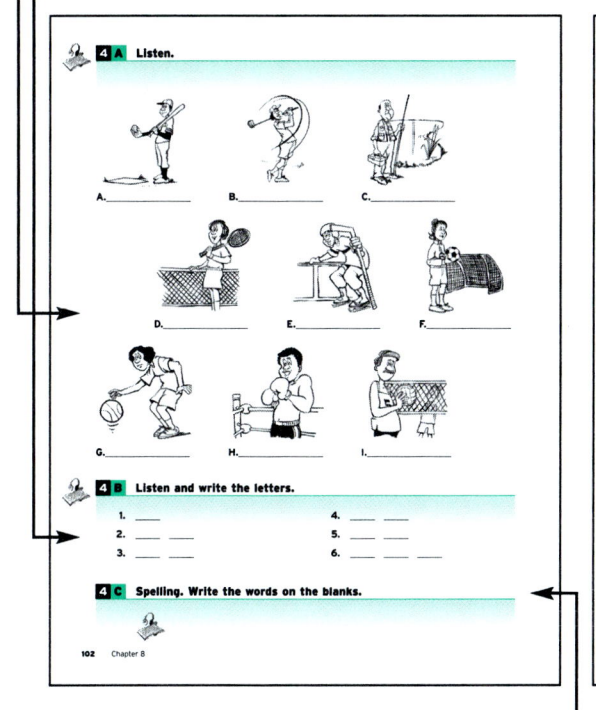

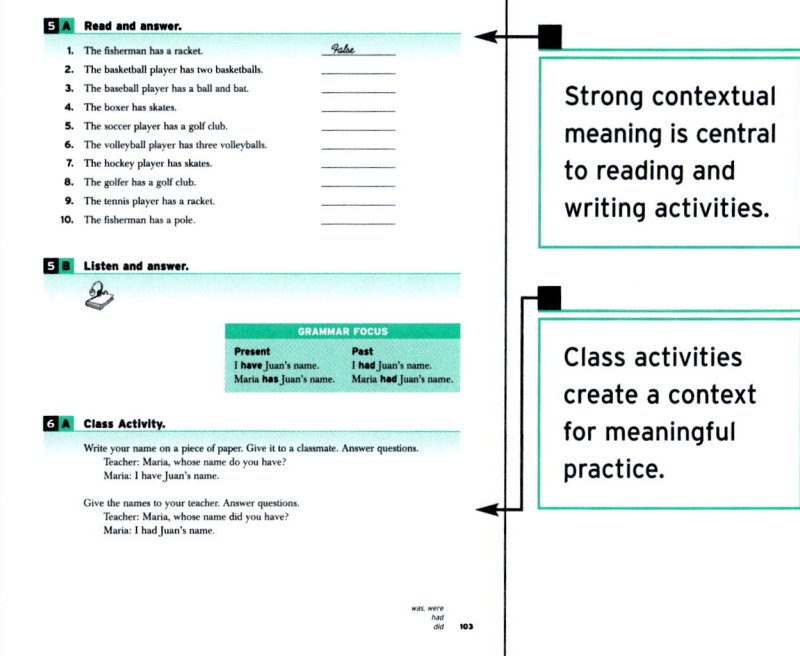

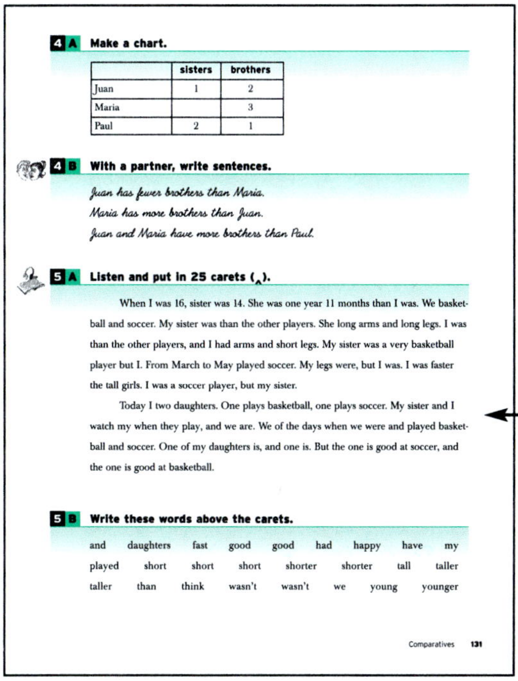

Overview **vii**

The Basics

Date 08/25/08

LESSON 1
numbers

1 A Listen to the numbers.

0   1   2   3   4   5   6   7   8   9   10

1 B Listen and circle.

1. 1   (2)   3
2. (6)   7   8
3. 0 1 (0 7) 0 9
4. 2 3   2 6 (2 8)
5. 4 2   4 4 (4 7)
6. 3 2 3 (3 5 8) 3 8 5
7. 5 0 7 7 0 5 (0 5 7)
8. (6 8 9) 9 8 6 8 6 9
9. 4 1 3 2 2 1 3 4 (3 2 1 4)
10. 7 0 6 4 (4 6 7 0) 0 6 4 7

2 Listen and write. + plus, = equals, - minus, x times

1. 2 + __2__ = __4__.
2. __4__ + 5 = __9__.
3. __7__ + __3__ = 10.
4. 8 - __6__ = __2__.
5. __9__ - 3 = __6__.

6. __10__ - __8__ = 2.
7. 3 x __2__ = __6__.
8. __2__ x 5 = __10__.
9. 10 ÷ __2__ = __5__.
10. __9__ ÷ 3 = __3__.

2   The Basics

Phone numbers   Date 08/26/08

3 Listen and write.

A.
1. 828 – 5791
2. 527 – 5172
3. 452 – 9555
4. 378 – 4391
5. 820 – 7331
6. 717 – 4396
7. 473 – 3001
8. 242 – 0409
9. 921 – 0335
10. 365 – 5061

B.
1. 482 – 1913
2. 590 – 6473
3. 225 – 0057
4. 481 – 1299
5. 466 – 0900
6. 267 – 4632
7. 561 – 1540
8. 768 – 9334
9. 531 – 8222
10. 489 – 8070

4 Listen and write.

A.
1. 205 – 939 – 9934
2. 334 – 609 – 3540
3. 907 – 339 – 6231
4. 870 – 486 – 6592
5. 707 – 942 – 0954
6. 859 – 862 – 8684
7. 651 – 219 – 5953
8. 406 – 297 – 2655
9. 862 – 352 – 4918
10. 575 – 992 – 3568

B.
1. 303 – 562 – 5881
2. 785 – 233 – 0217
3. 801 – 946 – 8485
4. 989 – 519 – 2255
5. 701 – 438 – 3238
6. 307 – 448 – 3496
7. 916 – 325 – 6640
8. 780 – 246 – 2327
9. 506 – 764 – 3623
10. 250 – 387 – 0238

Numbers 3

LESSON 2

alphabet

1 A Listen to the alphabet.

| A | B | C | D | E | F | G | H | I | J | K | L | M |
| N | O | P | Q | R | S | T | U | V | W | X | Y | Z |

1 B Listen and circle.

1. C   (D)   E
2. T   U   (V)
3. (A B)   A E   A U
4. M A   M O   (M N)
5. B L   (C H)   F R
6. I N G   G H T   (T C H)
7. E S S   (A N T)   E N T
8. (C H E E)   S H O U   T H R O
9. M E N T   S L E E   (O U N D)
10. A N C E   I B L E   (A N K S)

1 C Listen and circle.

1. A (B) C D E F G H I J K L M N O P Q R S (T) U V W X Y Z
2. A B C (D) E F G H I J K L M N (O) P Q R S T U V W X Y Z
3. A B C D E (F) G H I J K L (M) N O P Q R S (T) U V W X Y Z
4. A B C D (E) F G H I J K L M (N) O P Q R S T U V (W) X Y Z
5. (A) B C D E F G (H) I J K L M N (O) P Q R S T U V W X (Y) Z
6. A B C D (E) F G H I J K L (M) N O (P) Q R S T (U) V W X Y Z
7. A B C D E F G H (I) J K L M N O P Q R S T U V W X Y (Z)
8. (A) B C D E F G H (I) J K L M N (O) P Q R S T (U) V W X Y Z
   vowels
9. A B C D E F G H (I) J K L M N O P Q R S T U V W (X) Y Z
10. A B (C) D E F G H I J K L M N O P (Q) R S T U V W X (Y) Z

4   The Basics

2 A Listen and write.

1. T _W_ O = 2
2. T E _N_ = 10
3. _S_ _I_ X = 6
4. _O_ N _E_ = 1
5. _Z_ E _R O_ = 0
6. _N_ _I_ N _E_ = 9
7. _F O U_ R = 4
8. F _I_ _V_ _E_ = 5
9. T _H R E E_ = 3
10. _S E V E_ N = 7
11. _E I G H_ T = 8

2 B Listen and write your classmates' names.

That	Lwin	Rosalie	Hamilton
Kyaw	Oo	Cing	Lun
Kriss	Mattoo	Mohomed	Wariyow Somalia
Kriss	nasay		
Joanne	Cearbaugh		
Sa	ta		
Ei	Mer		
Marria	nauro		
Faith	duly		
Thanawot			
Jewel	duly		
Maw	Seh		
Charyo	Law		
Charly	Vazque		
Patrica			

Alphabet 5

1 To be

LESSON 1

there is, there are
is there?, are there?

1 A Listen.

Sunday
Monday
Tuesday
Wednesday
Thursday
Friday
Saturday

MAY

Sunday	Monday	Tuesday	Wednesday	Thursday	Friday	Saturday
		1	2	3	4	5
6	7	8	9	10	11	12

1 B Read and answer.

1. Are there seven letters in *Sunday*? No
2. Are there eight letters in *Thursday*? Yes
3. Are there two *a*'s in *Saturday*? yes
4. Are there two *d*'s in *Wednesday*? yes
5. Is there one *a* in *Monday*? yes
6. Is there one *s* in *Tuesday*? yes
7. Is there one *e* in *Wednesday*? no
8. Are there two *i*'s in *Friday*? no
9. Are there two *u*'s in *Tuesday*? no
10. Is there one *o* in *Monday*? yes
11. Is there one *r* in *Thursday*? yes
12. Are there two *s*'s in *Sunday*? no

2 A Listen and write the days of the week.

Sunday
Monday
Tuesday
Wednesday
Thursday
Friday
Saturday
} Days of the week.

2 B Listen and write *Yes* or *No*.

1. no
2. yes
3. yes
4. yes
5. yes
6. yes
7. no
8. no
9. no
10. yes
11. yes
12. no

6 Chapter 1

> **GRAMMAR FOCUS**
>
> **Singular**
> There **is** one *o* in *Monday*.
>
> **Plural**
> There **are** two *e*'s in *Wednesday*.

3 Write.

1. There *is* one *e* in *Tuesday*.
2. There *are* six letters in *Sunday*.
3. There is one *h* in *Thursday*.
4. There are nine letters in *Wednesday*.
5. There is one *i* in *Friday*.
6. There are six letters in *Sunday*, *Monday*, and *Friday*.
7. There is one *m* in *Monday*.
8. There are two *a*'s in *Saturday*.
9. There is one *u* in *Sunday*, *Tuesday*, *Thursday*, and *Saturday*.
10. There are eight letters in *Thursday* and *Saturday*.

4 A Spell your family name to your class. Write classmates' family names.

Garcia	~~Navorro~~	~~Shem~~	~~Oo~~
Chin	~~July~~	Kaercharh	~~Hattoo~~ ~~Wa Say~~
Martinez	~~Law~~	Lwin	Law
Choi	Vazquez	Aye	Cearbaugh

4 B With a partner, put the names in alphabetical order.

Chin
Choi
Garcia
Martinez

1. Aye
2. Cearbaugh
3. July
4. Kaercharh
5. Law
6. Lwin
7. Lwin
8. Toa ~~Htoo~~
9. Toa ~~Say~~
10. Navorro
11. Oo
12. Shem
13. Vazquez

To be 7

LESSON 2

it is, they are
singular/plural

World Map

1 A Listen to the countries.

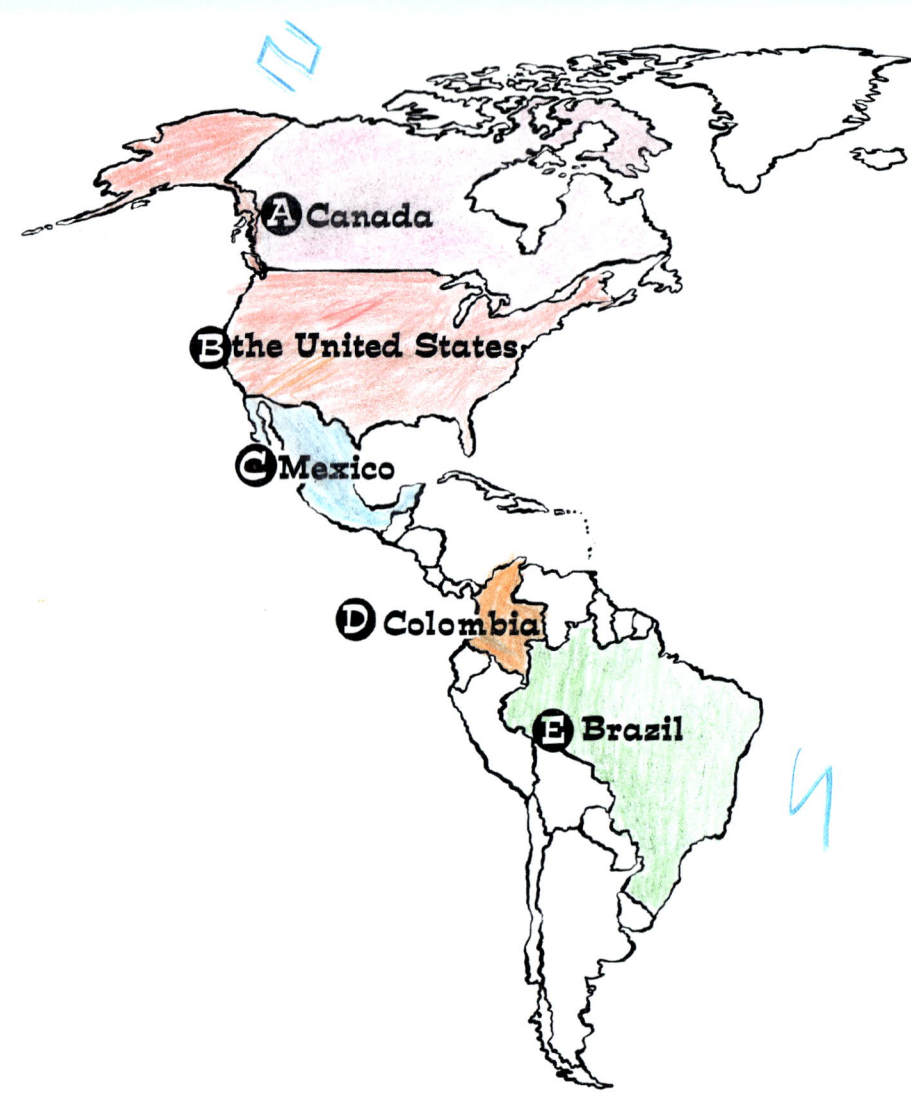

- Ⓐ Canada
- Ⓑ the United States
- Ⓒ Mexico
- Ⓓ Colombia
- Ⓔ Brazil

1 B Listen and write the letters.

1. B
2. H
3. L
4. C
5. J G
6. E D
7. A I
8. K F
9. G F H
10. A C B
11. L K J
12. D E C

Chapter 1

GRAMMAR FOCUS	
Brazil	Brazil**ian**
France	**French**
Japan	Japan**ese**

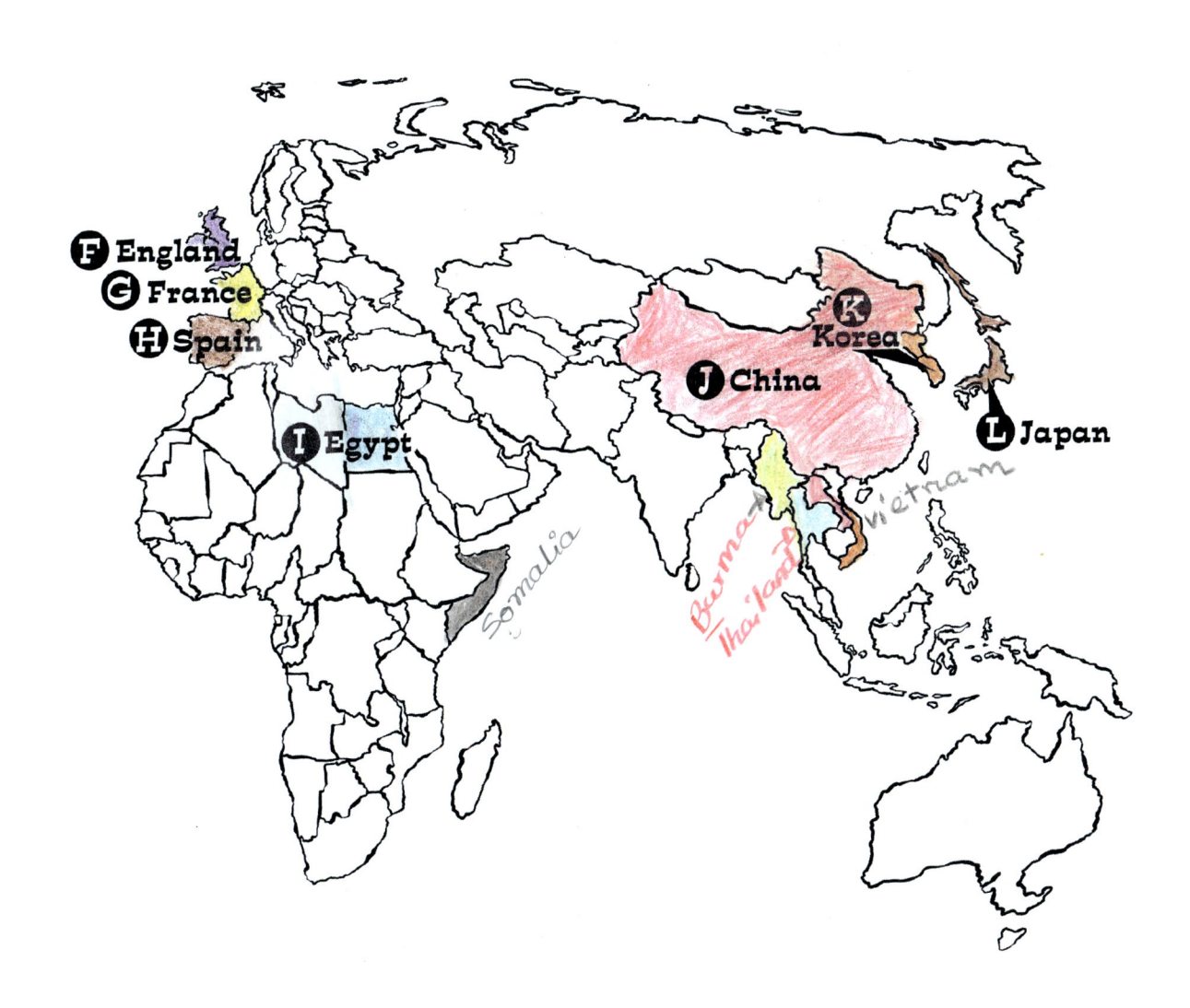

(Map with labels: F England, G France, H Spain, I Egypt, J China, K Korea, L Japan, Somalia, Burma, Thailand, Vietnam)

1 C Write the country.

1. Canadian — Canada
2. French — France
3. Korean — korea
4. Brazilian — Brazil
5. Egyptian — egypt
6. Colombian — Colombia

7. Japanese — Japan
8. Mexican — Mexico
9. Chinese — china
10. Spanish — Spain
11. English — England
12. American — America

Burmese — Burma
Vietnamese — Vietnam
Thai — Thailand
Somalian — Somalia

To be 9

2 A Listen to the cities.

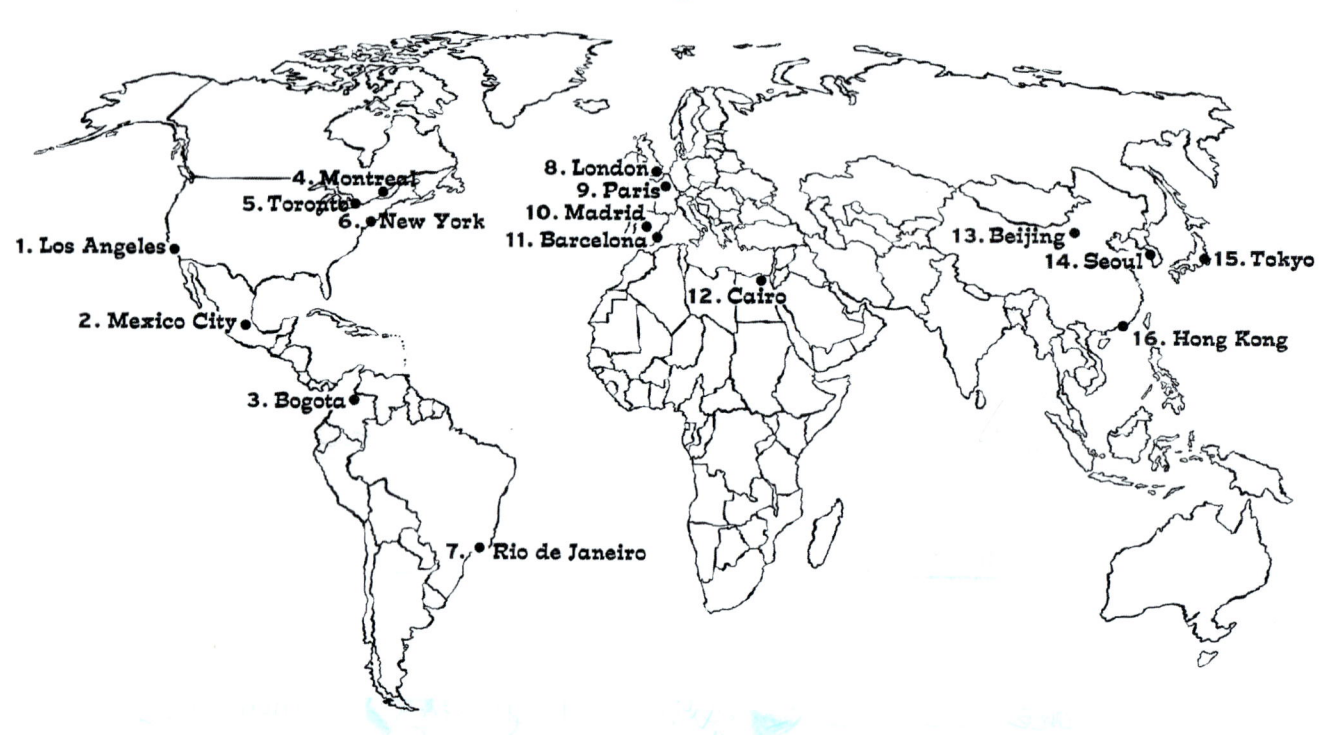

"World Map"

1. Los Angeles
2. Mexico City
3. Bogota
4. Montreal
5. Toronto
6. New York
7. Rio de Janeiro
8. London
9. Paris
10. Madrid
11. Barcelona
12. Cairo
13. Beijing
14. Seoul
15. Tokyo
16. Hong Kong

GRAMMAR FOCUS

Singular	Plural
a Chinese cit**y**	Chinese cit**ies**
an American cit**y**	American cit**ies**

2 B Read and write.

1. a Brazilian city — Rio de Janeiro
2. a Japanese city — Tokyo
3. a French city — Paris
4. two American cities — New York, Los Angeles
5. an Egyptian city — Cairo
6. two Chinese cities — Beijing, Hong Kong
7. a Korean city — Seoul
8. two Canadian cities — Montreal, Toronto
9. an English city — London
10. two Spanish cities — Madrid, Barcelona

3 A Read and answer.

1. Is Tokyo a Japanese city? — _Yes_
2. Is New York a Mexican city? — _No_
3. Is Bogota a Colombian city? — _yes_
4. Are Beijing and Hong Kong Chinese cities? — _yes_
5. Are Madrid and Barcelona French cities? — _no_
6. Are Los Angeles and New York American cities? — _yes_
7. Is Cairo a Chinese city? — _no_
8. Is London a Spanish city? — _no_
9. Are Toronto and Montreal Canadian cities? — _yes_
10. Is Rio de Janeiro an Egyptian city? — _no_

3 B Listen and answer.

GRAMMAR FOCUS

Singular		Plural	Singular		Plural
letter	+ s	letter**s**	city	− y + ies	cit**ies**
week		week**s**	country		countr**ies**

3 C With a partner, write sentences.

1. Seoul
   Seoul is a Korean city.
2. Barcelona and Madrid
   Barcelona and Madrid are Spanish cities.
3. Tokyo
   Tokyo is a Japanese city.
4. New York and Los Angeles _are American cities._
5. Paris
   is a French city.
6. Beijing and Hong Kong
   are chinese cities.
7. London
   is an english city.
8. Cairo
   is an Egyptian city.
9. Montreal and Toronto
   are canadian cities.
10. Mexico City
    is a Mexican city.
11. Rio de Janeiro
    is a Brazilian city.
12. Madrid and Barcelona
    are Spanish cities.

LESSON 3

subject pronouns with *to be*
contractions and negatives with *to be*
questions with *to be*

1 A   Practice the pronouns.

I

we

you

you
(plural)

he

she

they

12   Chapter 1

GRAMMAR FOCUS

Statement	Question	Statement	Question
I am American.	**Am I** American?	**We are** American.	**Are we** American?
You are American.	**Are you** American?	**You are** American.	**Are you** American?
He is American.	**Is he** American?	**They are** American.	**Are they** American?
She is American.	**Is she** American?		
It is American.	**Is it** American?		

1 B Write questions.

1. She is Korean. _Is she Korean?_
2. We are Spanish. _Are we Spanish?_
3. You are Canadian. _Are you Canadian?_
4. We are Brazilian. _Are we Brazilian?_
5. He is Mexican. _Is he Mexican?_
6. She is French. _Is she French?_
7. I am Colombian. _Am I Colombian?_
8. They are Japanese. _Are they Japanese?_
9. You are Egyptian. _Are you Egyptian?_
10. He is Chinese. _Is he Chinese?_
11. They are English. _Are they English?_
12. It is American. _Is it American?_

If, she likes pizza. Change to Does she like pizza?

2 A Listen.

1
2
3
4
5
6
7
8
Angela - canadian
Mark canadian
Sam American
Sarah American
Miguel mexican
Rosa mexican
Ferrand colombia
Paulo - Brazilian

2 B Read and answer.

1. Is Ming Chinese? *Yes, he is.*
2. Are Mark and Angela Mexican? *No, they aren't.*
3. Are Rosa and Miguel Spanish? no, they aren't.
4. Is Li French? no, she isn't.
5. Is Sam American? yes, he is.
6. Is Paulo Japanese? no, he isn't.

GRAMMAR FOCUS

Is Paulo Brazilian?	Yes, he **is**.
Is Keiko Spanish?	No, she **isn't**.
Are Rosa and Miguel Mexican?	Yes, they **are**.
Are Rosa and Miguel Colombian?	No, they **aren't**.

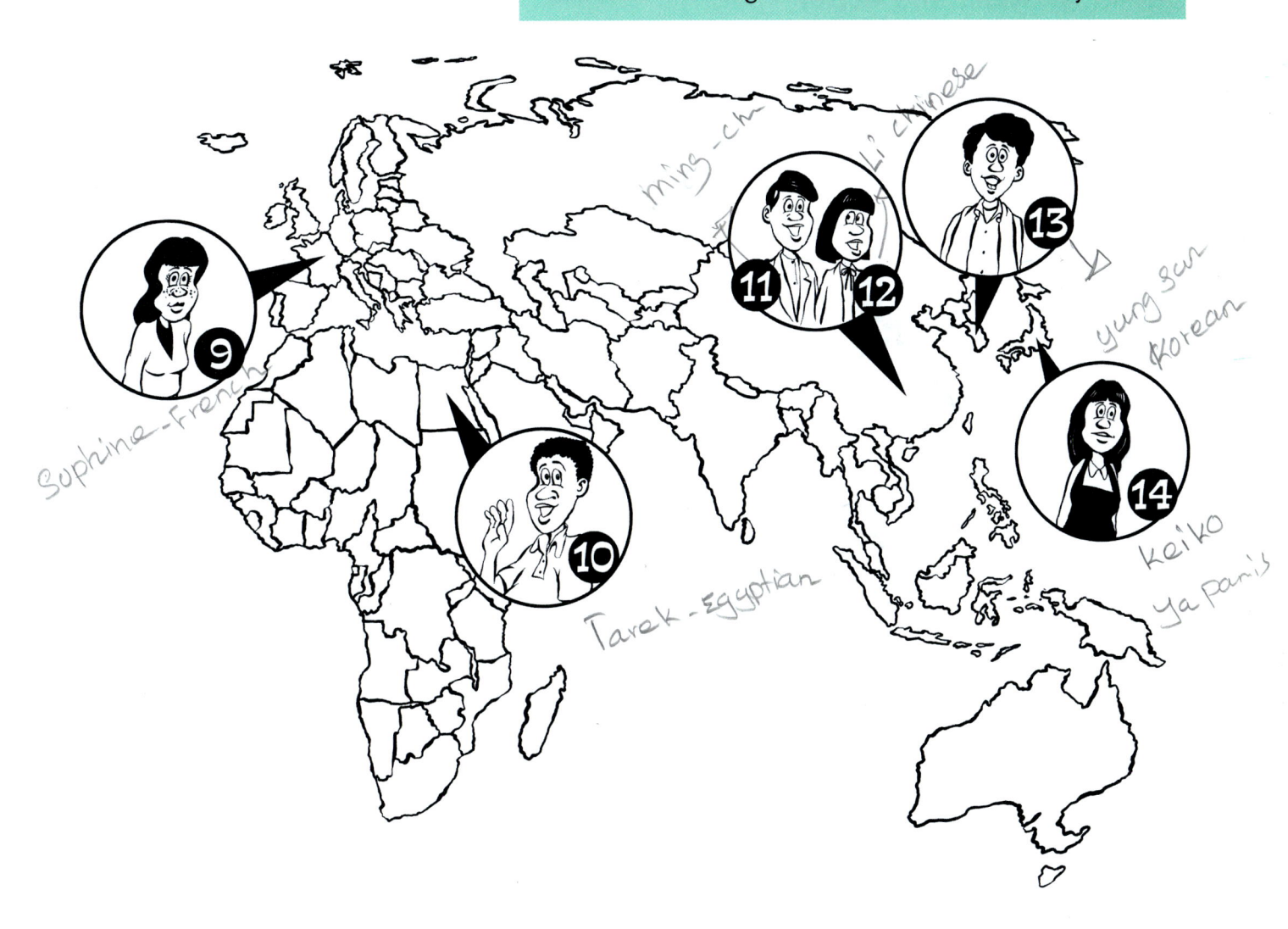

(map with handwritten annotations: Sophine–French, Tarek–Egyptian, ming-ch..., Li chinese, yung sun Korean, keiko Japanis)

7. Are Li and Ming Spanish?   *no, they aren't.*
8. Is Tarek Egyptian?   *yes, he is.*
9. Is Yung Sun English?   *no, he isn't.*
10. Are Sara and Sam Brazilian?   *no, they aren't.*

2 C Listen and write.

To be 15

LESSON 4

questions with *to be*
short answers with *to be*

1   A   Read and write.

1. Are you French? — *No, I'm not. I'm Colombian.*

2. Are you Canadian? — *Yes, I am. I'm Canadian.*

3. Are you Brazilian? — no, I'm not. I'm Japenese

4. Are you Mexican? — yes, we are. we're mexican

5. Is he Egyptian? — yes, he is. he's egyptian

16   Chapter 1

6. Are they Chinese?   yes, they are. they're chinese.

7. Is she Korean?   No, she isn't. she's French.

8. Is it American?   yes, it is. it's American.

GRAMMAR FOCUS

I am not.	= I'm not.		
You are not.	= You're not.	= You aren't.	
He is not.	= He's not.	= He isn't.	
She is not.	= She's not.	= She isn't.	
It is not.	= It's not.	= It isn't.	
We are not.	= We're not.	= We aren't.	
You are not.	= You're not.	= You aren't.	
They are not.	= They're not.	= They aren't.	

---

1 B Take a card with the name of a country. Answer questions.

Are you French?
No, I'm not.

Is he Colombian?
Yes, he is.

2 A Listen.

Paris London Beijing etc.	Canada Spain Japan etc.	A E I O U

A _cities_   B _countries_   C _vowels_

B C D F G H J K L M N P Q R S T V W X Y Z	2 4 6 8 10	1 3 5 7 9

D _consonants_   E _even numbers_   F _odd numbers_

2 B Listen and write the letters.

1. B
2. E
3. D C

4. B A
5. E F C
6. A B D

2 C Spelling. Write the words on the blanks.

cities
countries
vowels
consonants
even numbers
odd numbers

3 A Read and answer.

1. Is Madrid a city? — _Yes, it is._
2. Are Tokyo and Seoul countries? — _No, they aren't._
3. Are 4 and 6 even numbers? — _yes, they are._
4. Is London a country? — _no, it isn't._

18 Chapter 1

5. Is 7 an even number? _No, it isn't._
6. Are *A* and *E* consonants? _No, they aren't._
7. Are New York and Los Angeles cities? _Yes, they are._
8. Is *O* a vowel? _Yes, it is._
9. Are 5 and 9 odd numbers? _Yes, they are._

3 B Listen and write.

1. Yes, it is.
2. No, they aren't.
3. Yes, they are.
4. No, it isn't.
5. No, it isn't.
6. No, they aren't.
7. Yes, they are.
8. Yes, it is.
9. Yes, they are.

4 A Write questions and answers.

1. Los Angeles / country
   Is Los Angeles a country?   No, it isn't.

2. 5, 7, 9 / odd numbers
   Are 5, 7, 9 odd numbers?   Yes, they're.

3. New York and Toronto / cities
   Are New York and Toronto cities?   Yes, they're.

4. *O* / consonant
   Is O consonant?   No, it isn't.

5. Canada and Mexico / countries
   Are Canada and Mexico countries?   Yes, they're.

6. 1 and 3 / even numbers
   Are 1 and 3 even numbers?   No, they aren't.

7. *F* and *G* / vowels
   Are F and G vowels?   No, they aren't.

8. Japan and China / cities
   Are Japan and China cities?   No, they aren't.

9. *U* / vowel
   Is U vowel?   Yes, it is.

4 B With a partner, ask and answer questions.

Are 2, 4, and 6 even numbers?   Yes, they are.

2 Prepositions

LESSON 1
prepositions of place

1 A Listen.

A. _pencil_    B. _Pen_ 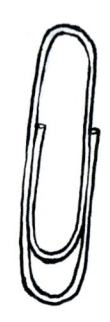   C. _Paper clip_ 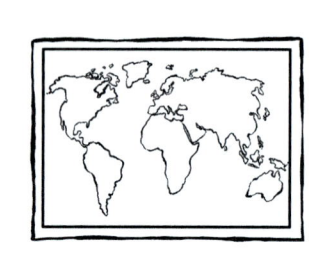   D. _Map_

E. _book_    F. _Sheet of paper_ 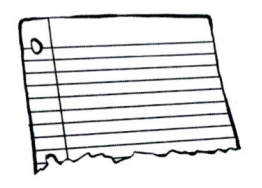   G. _half sheet of paper_

1 B Listen and write the letters.

1. _E_
2. _B_
3. _D_
4. _F_
5. _B A_
6. _G D_
7. _E A F_
8. _B C E_

1 C Spelling. Write the words on the blanks.

Percil   book
Pen   Sheet of paper
Paper clip   half sheet of paper.
Map

20 Chapter 2

2 A Listen.

A. The pencil is ___on___ the book.

B. The pencil is ___in___ the book.

C. The pencil is ___under___ the book.

D. The pencil is ___to the Right of___ the book.

E. The pencil is ___to the Left of___ the book.

F. The pencil is ___between___ the books.

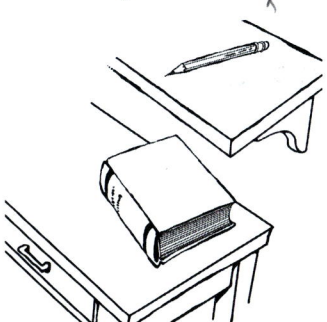

G. The pencil is ___above___ the book.

2 B Listen and write the letters.

1. _B_   2. _C_   3. _F_   4. _A_   5. _D_   6. _G_   7. _E_

2 C Spelling. Write the words on the blanks.

on
in
under
to the right of
to the left of
between
above

Prepositions   21

3 A Read and answer.

1. Is there a sheet of paper under the book? _Yes_
2. Are there two pens to the left of the book? _No_
3. Is there a half sheet of paper on the book? _No_
4. Is there a map above the book? _yes_
5. Is there a pencil to the right of the book? _yes_
6. Are there two pencils and a paper clip on the book? _yes_
7. Is there a half sheet of paper in the book? _yes_
8. Is there a paper clip between the pencils? _yes_

3 B Listen to the commands.

1. Put a sheet of paper under your book.
2. Put a half sheet of paper in your book.
3. Put a pen to the right of your book.
4. Put a pencil to the left of your book.
5. Put a half sheet of paper on your book.
6. Put a paper clip between the book and the half sheet of paper.

4 A Listen and put in 9 carets (∧).

The pen is <ins>under</ins> the book. The half sheet of paper is <ins>on</ins> the book. The map is <ins>above</ins> the book. The pencil is <ins>in</ins> the book. The sheet of paper is <ins>to</ins> the left <ins>of</ins> the book. The paper clip is <ins>to</ins> the right <ins>of</ins> the book. The book is <ins>between</ins> the sheet of paper and the paper clip.

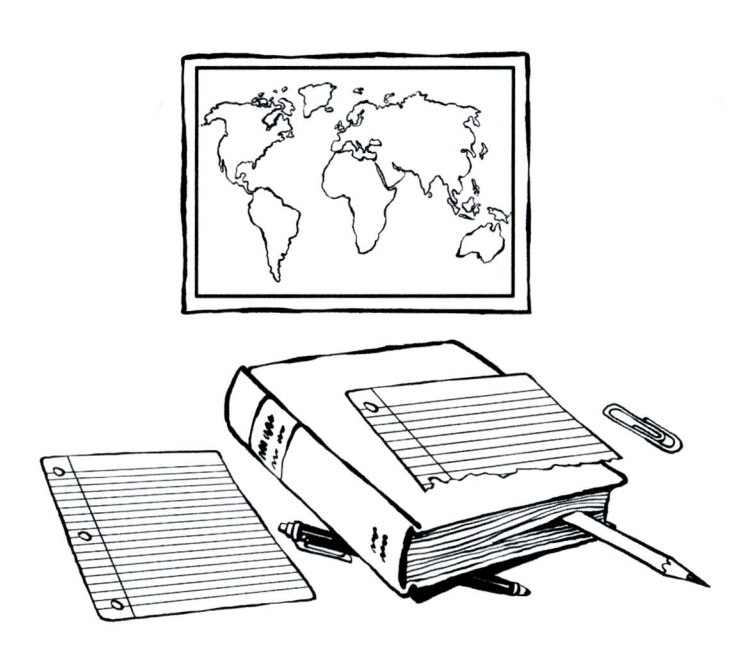

4 B Write these words above the carets.

above   between   in   of   of   on   to   to   under

The Pen is under the book. The half sheet of paper is on the book. The map is above the book. The pencil is in the book. The sheet of paper is to the left of the book. The paper clip is to the right of the book. The book is between the sheet of paper and the paper clip.

Prepositions   23

LESSON 2

prepositions of place
possessive adjectives
Who is . . . ?

1 A   Listen.

A. _nose_   B. _Eyes_   C. _cheeks_   D. _Mouth_   E. _ears_

F. _hair_   G. _teeth_   H. _head_   I. _chin_   J. _neck_

1 B   Listen and write the letters.

1. _C_
2. _F_
3. _A_
4. _B_
5. _D_
6. _G_
7. _H_   _J_
8. _C_   _D_
9. _B_   _G_
10. _A_   _E_
11. _F_   _B_   _C_
12. _D_   _J_   _G_

1 C   Spelling. Write the words on the blanks.

nose   teeth
Eyes   head
cheeks   chin
Mouth   neck
ears
hair

GRAMMAR FOCUS

"My book."    "Your book."

24   Chapter 2

2 A Read and answer.

1. Are your teeth in your mouth? 1. _Yes_
2. Are your eyes under your nose? 2. _No_
3. Is your nose between your cheeks? 3. _Yes_
4. Is your hair on your head? 4. _Yes_
5. Are your ears above your eyes? 5. _No_
6. Is your head between your ears? 6. _Yes_
7. Is your right eye above your left cheek? 7. _No_
8. Is your nose above your mouth? 8. _Yes_
9. Is your neck under your chin? 9. _Yes_
10. Is your nose to the left of your right eye? 10. _Yes_

2 B Listen and write.

1. yes   5. no   9. yes
2. no   6. yes   10. yes
3. yes   7. no
4. yes   8. yes

2 C Write the prepositions.

under   above   between   in   on   to the left of   to the right of

1. My nose is _between_ my cheeks.
2. My teeth are _in_ my mouth.
3. My hair is _on_ my head.
4. My mouth is _above_ my chin.
5. My head is _between_ my ears.
6. My neck is _under_ my chin.
7. My mouth is _between_ my chin and nose.
8. My left eye is _to the left of_ my nose.
9. My chin is _above_ my neck.
10. My right cheek is _under_ my right eye.
11. My nose is _to the left of_ my right eye.
12. My mouth is _under_ my nose.
13. My left eye is _above_ my left cheek.
14. My left cheek is _to the right of_ my left ear.

Prepositions 25

3 A Listen.

[Seating chart with 9 students at desks in 3 rows:
Row 1 (back): Tarek, Rosa, Yung Sun
Row 2 (middle): Paulo, Sophie, Miguel
Row 3 (front): Li, Keiko, Fernando]

GRAMMAR FOCUS

Sophie is **in front of** Rosa.   Sophie is **next to** Paulo.
Sophie is **behind** Keiko.   Sophie is **next to** Miguel.

3 B Read and answer.

1. Who is in front of Sophie? _Keiko is._
2. Who is next to Paulo? _Sophie is_
3. Who is in front of Miguel? _Fernando is_
4. Who is behind Paulo? _Tarek is_
5. Who is in front of Yung Sun? _Miguel is_
6. Who is next to Li? _Keiko is_
7. Who is behind Fernando? _Miguel is_
8. Who is next to Tarek? _Rosa is_
9. Who is in front of Rosa? _Sophie is_
10. Who is behind Miguel? _Yung Sun_

26 Chapter 2

4 A Fill in the seating chart for your class.

```
                    Teacher Joanne
┌──────┬──┬─────────┬──────────┬──┬──────────┐
│SarAye│  │ CharLy  │kristellnaHtoo│  │Eh ku thay│
├──────┼──┼─────────┼──────────┼──┼──────────┤
│Marria│  │ Kyaw oo │ Charyo   │  │Lah You kyi│
├──────┼──┼─────────┼──────────┼──┼──────────┤
│Jewel │  │Mohamed  │  Maw     │  │krisstellnasay│
├──────┼──┼─────────┼──────────┼──┼──────────┤
│Marta │  │         │          │  │ Cing     │
├──────┼──┼─────────┼──────────┼──┼──────────┤
│Faith │  │         │          │  │The² Lwin │
├──────┼──┼─────────┼──────────┼──┼──────────┤
│ RiLa │  │         │          │  │Tay Zaw   │
├──────┼──┼─────────┼──────────┼──┼──────────┤
│      │  │         │          │  │Thanawt   │
├──────┼──┼─────────┼──────────┼──┼──────────┤
│Vinlue│  │         │          │  │ Vlady    │
└──────┴──┴─────────┴──────────┴──┴──────────┘
  Clock                                  Window
door
```

4 B With a partner, ask and answer questions.

Who is next to Maria?   Juan is.

krisstellna Htoo is in Front of charyo.
Charyo is behind krisstellna Htoo.
kyaw oo is next to charyo.

That² Lwin is next to tay Zaw.
Charyo is in Front of Maw.
I'm next to Maria.
Maw is behind charyo.
Jewel is next to Marria.

Optional Activity. Write ten sentences about your class.

I am in front of Maria.

Maria is next to Juan.

Prepositions   27

LESSON 3

before, after, between
What is . . . ?, What are . . . ?

1A Listen.

A B C D E F G H I J K L M N O P Q R S T U V W X Y Z

A B C D E F G H I J K L M N O P Q R S T U V W X Y Z
a b c d e f g h i j k l m n o p q r s t u v w x y z

GRAMMAR FOCUS

A   B   C
B is **after** A. B is **before** C.
B is **between** A and C.

1B Read and answer.

1. Is B after A? — Yes
2. Is L after K? — yes
3. Is R before S? — yes
4. Is W after V? — yes
5. Is Z before Y? — no
6. Is G after F? — yes
7. Is H after I? — no
8. Is N before M? — no
9. Is Q before P? — no
10. Is J before K? — yes

1C Write the alphabet. Listen and answer the questions.

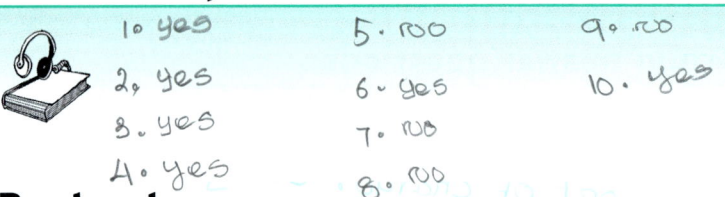

1. yes
2. yes
3. yes
4. yes
5. no
6. yes
7. no
8. no
9. no
10. yes

1D Read and answer.

1. What's the letter between A and C? — B
2. What are the letters between L and O? — M N
3. What are the letters between P and S? — Q R
4. What's the letter after S? — T
5. What's the letter before K? — J
6. What are the letters between D and H? — E F G
7. What's the letter between T and V? — U
8. What are the letters before D? — A B C
9. What's the letter after I? — J
10. What are the letters after W? — X Y Z

28 Chapter 2

2 A Listen.

10 11 12 13 14 15 16 17 18 19 20

> **GRAMMAR FOCUS**
> What is = What's

2 B Read and answer.

1. What's the number after 10?   _11_
2. What's the number before 19?   _18_
3. What's the number between 14 and 16?   _15_
4. What's the number between 11 and 13?   _12_
5. What's the number after 14?   _15_
6. What's the number before 11?   _10_
7. What are the numbers between 14 and 17?   _15, 16_
8. What are the numbers before 3?   _1, 2_
9. What are the numbers after 15 and before 18?   _16, 17_
10. What are the numbers before 14 and after 11?   _13, 12_

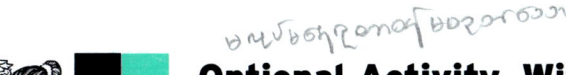

Optional Activity. With a partner, read the questions of 2B.

> **GRAMMAR FOCUS**
> **Years**
> 1917 = nineteen-seventeen
> 1907 = nineteen-oh-seven   (0 = oh, not zero)

2 C Listen and circle.

1. 1917 (1916) 1915
2. 1811 1812 (1813)
3. 1720 (1721) 1722
4. (1909) 1908 1906
5. 1215 (1214) 1213
6. 1212 1202 (1222)
7. (1121) 1125 1129
8. 1001 (1015) 1010
9. 1317 (1312) 1311
10. (1602) 1612 1622

Prepositions   **29**

3 A Listen.

10   20   30   40   50   60   70   80   90   100

GRAMMAR FOCUS

Prices

$55.95 = fifty-five dollars and ninety-five cents = fifty-five ninety-five

---

3 B Listen and circle.

1. 26.99   (26.95)   26.59
2. (33.44)   33.40   34.40
3. 42.81   41.81   (48.41)
4. 76.14   74.16   (76.16)
5. 88.11   (88.12)   88.13

6. 91.02   (92.01)   (91.01)
7. 59.31   (59.13)   13.59
8. 62.69   (62.96)   69.62
9. (12.04)   12.40   12.44
10. 11.03   3.11   (11.02)

3 C Read and answer.

1. What's the number after 29? — 30
2. What's the number before 80? — 70
3. What are the numbers between 50 and 53? — 51, 52
4. What's the number between 88 and 90? — 89
5. What are the numbers before 30 and after 27? — 29, 28
6. What are the numbers after 40 and before 43? — 41, 42
7. What's the number before 100? — 99
8. What's the number after 59? — 60
9. What's the number after 99? — 100
10. What are the numbers between 110 and 113? — 111, 112

4A Listen and spell.

1. 11   _eleven_
2. 12   _twelve_
3. 13   _Thirteen_
4. 20   _Twenty_
5. 30   _Thirty_
6. 40   _Forty_
7. 50   _Fifty_
8. 60   _Sixty_
9. 70   _Seventy_
10. 80   _Eighty_
11. 90   _Ninety_
12. 100 _One hundred_

4B Read and write.

1. Are there 3 *e*'s in 11?   _Yes_
2. Is there a *t* after *w* in 12?   _No_
3. Are there 2 *t*'s in 13?   _yes_
4. Is there an *r* between *o* and *t* in 40?   _yes_
5. Are there 2 *n*'s in 20?   _no_
6. Is there a *y* before *t* in 50?   _no_
7. Is there a *ty* after *x* in 60?   _yes_
8. Are there 2 *e*'s between *t* and *n* in 13?   _yes_
9. Is there a *g* before *i* in 80?   _no_
10. Are there 2 *d*'s in 100?   _yes_

4C Listen and answer.

Prepositions 31

LESSON 4

prepositions of place
where is?, where are?

1 A **Listen and connect the numbers and letters.**

1 2 3 4 5 6 7 8 9 10 11 12 13 14 15 16 17 18 19 20 21 22 23 24 25 26

A B C D E F G H I J K L M N O P Q R S T U V W X Y Z

1 B **Read and answer.**

1. Is there a line from 9 to H?   *Yes*
2. Is there a line from 15 to N?   _____
3. Is there a line from 24 to W?   _____
4. Is there a line from 12 to L?   _____
5. Is there a line from 3 to D?   _____
6. Is there a line from 13 to O?   _____
7. Is there a line from 8 to I?   _____
8. Is there a line from 23 to X?   _____
9. Is there a line from 15 to Q?   _____
10. Is there a line from 10 to G?   _____

2 A Listen.

A. _without nose_   B. _without eyes_   C. _with a hat_

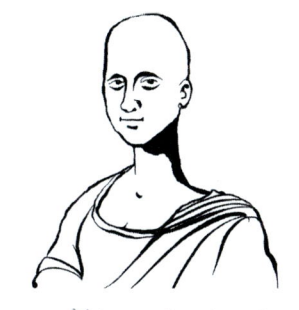

D. _without hair_   E. _with teeth_   F. _with glasses_

2 B Listen and write the letters.

1. ____
2. ____
3. ____
4. ____
5. ____

6. ____
7. ____ ____
8. ____ ____
9. ____ ____
10. ____ ____ ____

2 C Write under the pictures.

with a hat   without a nose

with glasses   without eyes

with teeth   without hair

Prepositions   33

3 A Listen.

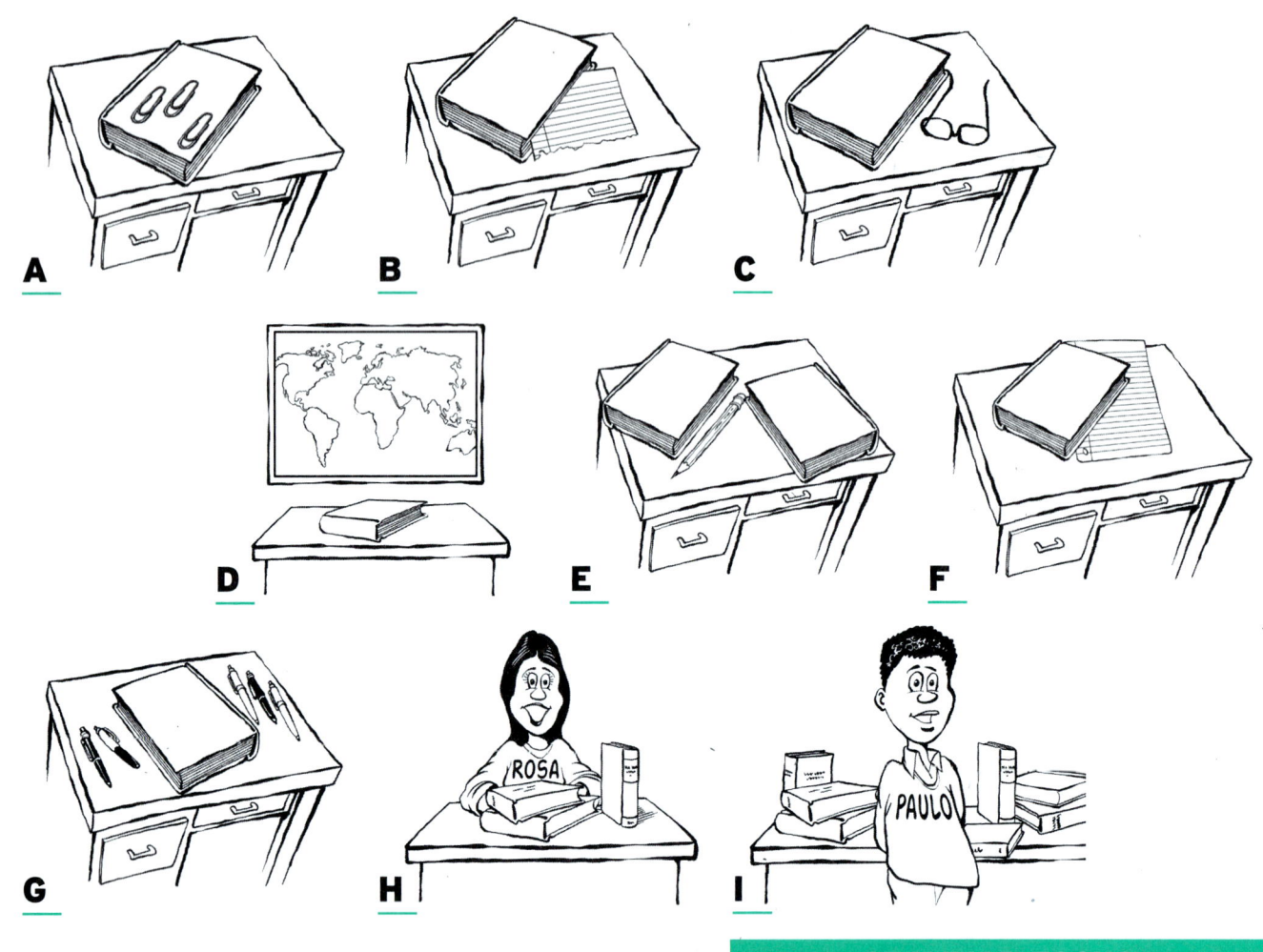

A | **B** | **C**

D | **E** | **F**

G | **H** (Rosa) | **I** (Paulo)

GRAMMAR FOCUS

Where
Where is the pencil?
It is **on the book.**

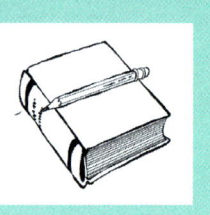

3 B Read and answer.

1. Where are the paper clips? — *They are on the book.*
2. Where is the sheet of paper? — *It is under the book.*
3. Where are the glasses? — They are on the table.
4. Where is the map? — It is above the table.
5. Where are the three books? — They are left of the paulo.

34 Chapter 2

6. Where is the half sheet of paper?   It is in the book.
7. Where are the seven books?   They are behind of Paulo.
8. Where is the pencil?   It is between the books.
9. Where are the two pens?   They are left of the book.

4 A Find these words. Circle.

| IN | AFTER | WITHOUT | BEFORE | WITH | ABOVE |
| BEHIND | UNDER | BETWEEN | FROM | ON | TO |

```
O V N T X W W R U A I W
A N G A H H E S H E A I
F R O M Y D R M V A W T
B M F W N T B D L E F H
R E T U C O E I P I X K
B V F L H M T A D B Q B
T M V O D K W F V B U E
L O C F R D E T A N R E
G E I P D E E F G V U
B E H I N D N R F O H E
W I T H O U T E B I Y T
H W E S O Z B A W N Y I
```

4 B With a partner, write the words you found in alphabetical order.

above   From
Behind   under
to   with
after   After
Between   on
Before   without

Prepositions 35

3 To have

LESSON 1

have, had
do and does with have

1 A Listen.

GRAMMAR FOCUS

Fernando has a book. Fernando**'s** book
Bill has a family. Bill**'s** family

A. Bill

B._____ C._____

D._____ E._____ F._____

G._____

H._____ I._____

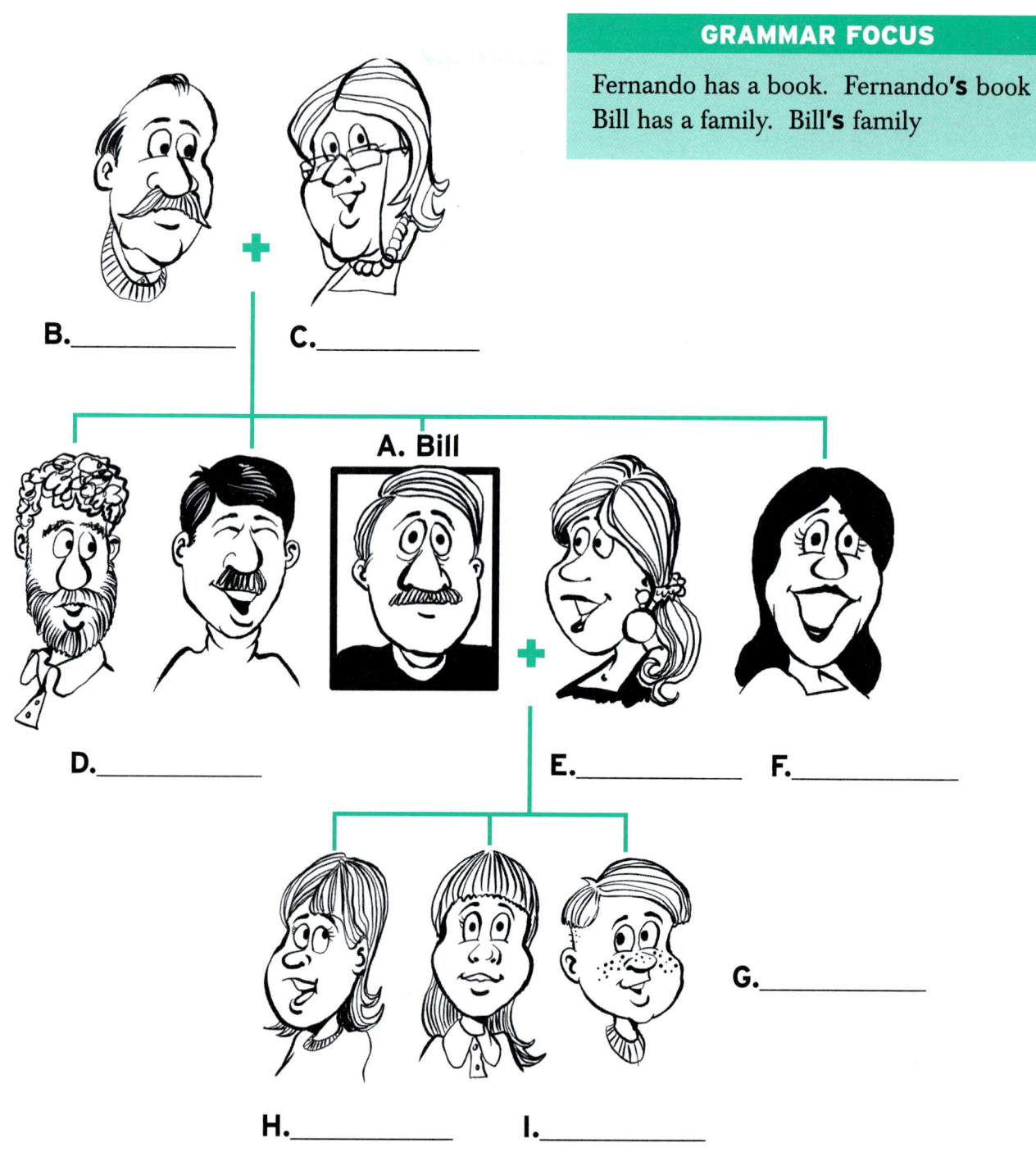

36 Chapter 3

1 B Listen and write the letters.

1. ____
2. ____
3. ____
4. ____
5. ____
6. ____
7. ____
8. ____
9. ____ ____
10. ____ ____
11. ____ ____ ____
12. ____ ____ ____

1 C Spelling. Write the words on the blanks.

> **GRAMMAR FOCUS**
>
> I **have** two eyes. We **have** two eyes.
> You **have** two eyes. You **have** two eyes.
> He **has** two eyes. They **have** two eyes.
> She **has** two eyes.
> It **has** two eyes.

1 D Read and answer.

1. Bill has a wife. — *True*
2. Bill has two sons. — *False*
3. Bill has two fathers. — ____
4. Bill has two sisters. — ____
5. Bill has one brother. — ____
6. Bill has three daughters. — ____
7. Bill has two sisters and one brother. — ____
8. Bill has two sons. — ____
9. Bill has three children. — ____
10. Bill's father has four children. — ____
11. Bill's wife has three children. — ____

1 E Listen and answer.

To have

2 Look and write. Use "I" or "We."

a big chin   big ears   a big head   a big mouth   a big nose   big cheeks   big eyes

1. *I have big eyes.*
2. *We have big cheeks.*
3. *I have a big nose.*
4. *We have big ears.*   
5. *I have a big head.*
6. *I have a big chin.*
7. *We have big eyes.*   
8. *I have big ears.*
9. *I have a big mouth.*

GRAMMAR FOCUS

Do and *Does* with *Have*

Statement	Question	Statement	Question
I have a book.	**Do** I have a book?	He has a book.	**Does** he have a book?
You have a book.	**Do** you have a book?	She has a book.	**Does** she have a book?
We have a book.	**Do** we have a book?	It has a book.	**Does** it have a book?
They have a book.	**Do** they have a book?		

3 A Class Activity. Write your classmates' names. Answer the questions.

"Juan, do you have brothers and sisters?"

"Yes, I have two brothers and one sister."

	Brothers	Sisters
Juan	2	1
_____	_____	_____
_____	_____	_____
_____	_____	_____
_____	_____	_____
_____	_____	_____
_____	_____	_____
_____	_____	_____
_____	_____	_____
_____	_____	_____
_____	_____	_____

GRAMMAR FOCUS

Do you have two sisters?   Yes, **I do**. = Yes, I have two sisters.
Does he have two sisters?   Yes, **he does**. = Yes, he has two sisters.

3 B Class Activity. Look at the chart and answer the questions.

Teacher: Who has two brothers and one sister?   Juan: I do.

Teacher: Who has two brothers and one sister?   Maria: Juan does.

To have 39

LESSON 2

do not, does not

> **GRAMMAR FOCUS**
>
> **Negative Statements**
>
> I have two brothers.　　　　I **do not** have two sisters.
> You have two brothers.　　　You **do not** have two sisters.
> We have two brothers.　　　We **do not** have two sisters.
> They have two brothers.　　They **do not** have two sisters.
>
> He has two brothers.　　　　　He **does not** have two sisters.
> She has two brothers.　　　　　She **does not** have two sisters.
> Bill Parker has two brothers.　Bill **does not** have two sisters.

1 Read and write.

1. Bill _has_ a sister.
2. Bill _does not have_ 20 sisters.
3. I _have_ an English book.
4. We _do not have_ 500 pencils.
5. You _have_ a wife.
6. She _does not have_ 145 maps.
7. I _have_ 2 noses.
8. We _do not have_ sheets of paper.
9. Bill _have_ 3 children.
10. They _do not have_ eyes and ears.
11. You _have_ 10 mothers.
12. They _do not have_ 900 paper clips.

Chapter 3

2 A Listen.

A.  _____ B.  _____ C. _____

D. 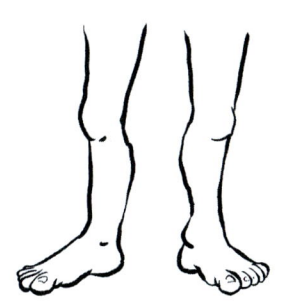 _____ E. 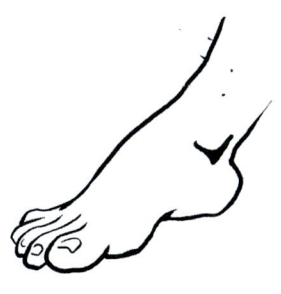 _____ F. 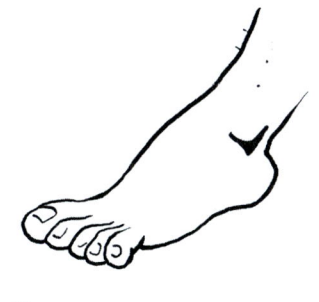 _____ G. _____

H. 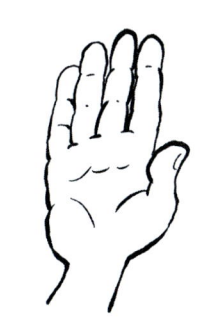 _____ I. 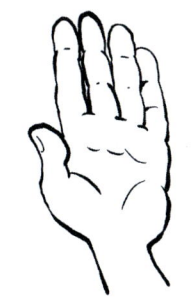 _____ J. _____

2 B Listen and write the letters.

1. ____
2. ____
3. ____
4. ____

5. ____
6. ____ ____
7. ____ ____ ____
8. ____ ____ ____

2 C Spelling. Write the words on the blanks.

To have   41

GRAMMAR FOCUS

Do you have four arms?   No, I **do not**. = No, I **don't**.
Does she have two heads? No, she **does not**. = No, she **doesn't**.

3 A Listen.

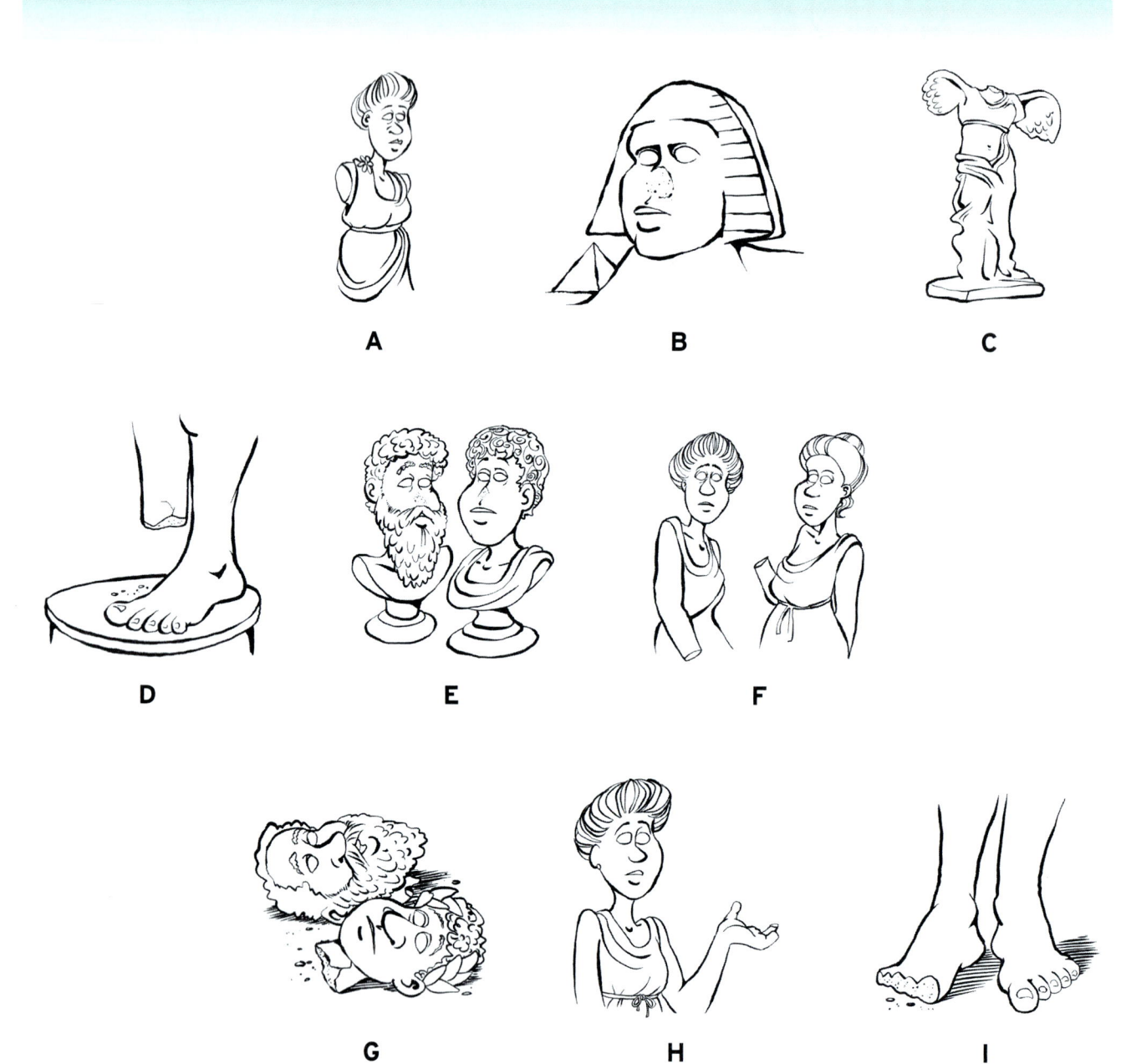

A

B

C

D

E

F

G

H

I

3 B Listen and write the letters.

1. _____
2. _____
3. _____
4. _____
5. _____ _____
6. _____ _____
7. _____ _____
8. _____ _____

42   Chapter 3

3 C Look, read, and write.

1. Does she have arms? — No, she doesn't.
2. Does she have a head? — Yes, she does.

3. Do they have arms? — yes, they do.
4. Do they have hands? — no, they don't.

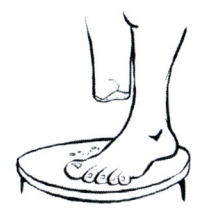

5. Does he have a right foot? — no, he doesn't.
6. Does he have a left foot? — yes, he does.

7. Do they have noses? — no, they don't.
8. Do they have ears? — yes, they does.

9. Do they have necks? — yes, they do.
10. Do they have bodies? — no, they don't.

11. Does she have a right ear? — yes, she does.
12. Does she have fingers? —

13. Does it have a nose? — no, It doesn't.
14. Does it have a head? — yes, It does.

15. Does she have a body? — yes, she does.
16. Does she have a head? — no, she doesn't.

To have

LESSON 3
possessive adjectives

1 A Listen.

George — Ida
B_____

Grace, Nina, James, Mary, Ron

C_____ D_____ E_____

Louis, Eric, A. Bill, Linda, Ann, Pablo

F_____

Carla, Emma, John, Steve, Laura

G_____ H_____

I_____

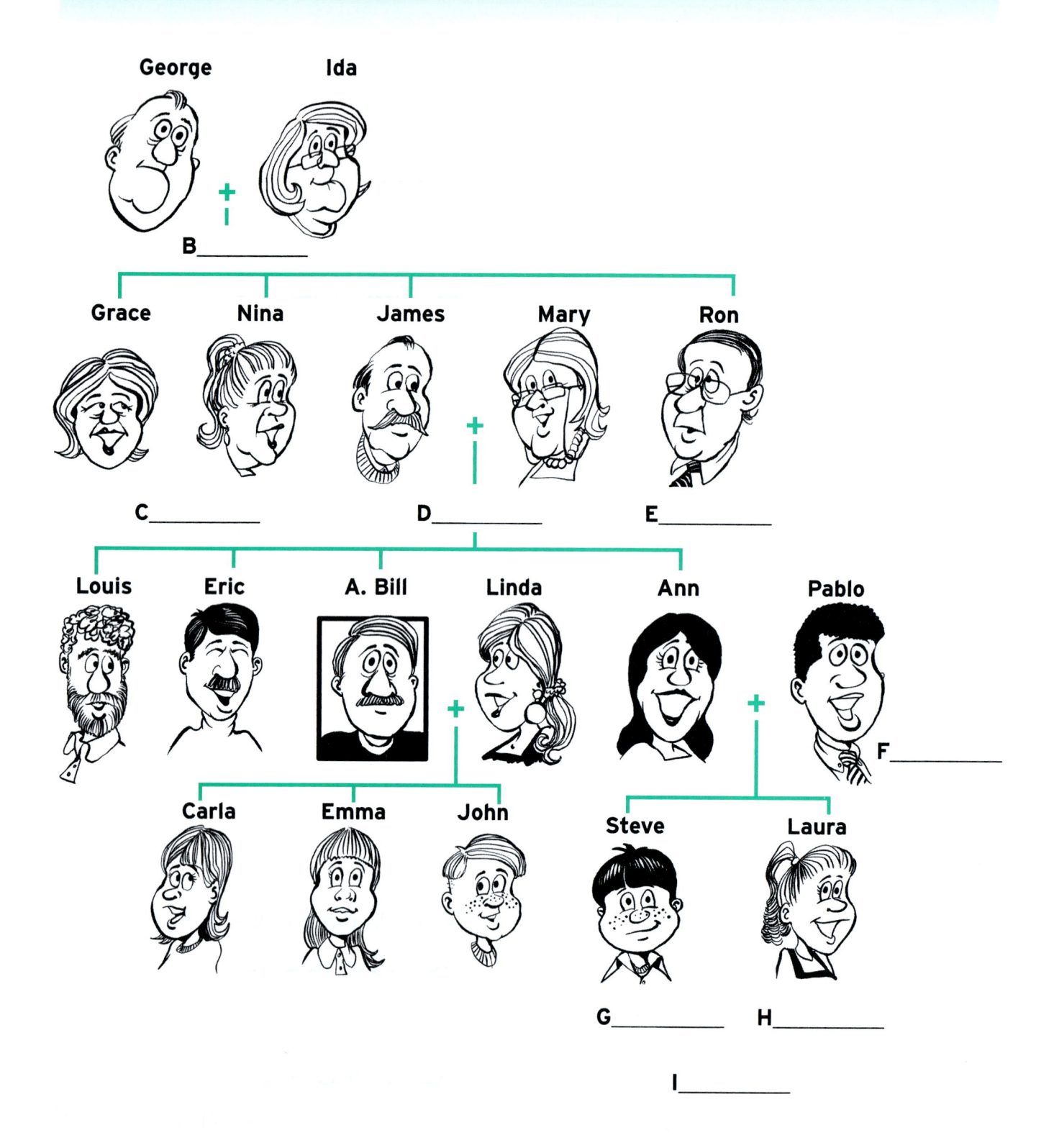

44   Chapter 3

GRAMMAR FOCUS

Bill has a son. **His** son is John.
Bill has 2 daughters. **His** daughters are Carla and Emma.

1 B Listen and write the letters.

1. ____
2. ____
3. ____
4. ____

5. ____ ____
6. ____ ____
7. ____ ____ ____
8. ____ ____ ____

1 C Spelling. Write the words on the blanks.

2 A Class Activity.

My name is . . . .

Your name is . . . . . .

His name is . . . .

Her name is . . . .

Our names are . . . . .

Their names are . . . .

GRAMMAR FOCUS

Possessive Adjectives

I have a Korean name. **My** name is Kim.
You have a French name. **Your** name is Sophie.
He has a Colombian name. **His** name is Fernando.
She has a Japanese name. **Her** name is Keiko.
It has an American name. **Its** name is Ford.
We have Chinese names. **Our** names are Ming and Li.
They have Mexican names. **Their** names are Rosa and Miguel.

To have

2 B Look, read, and answer.

1. Bill is their brother.   _True_

2. Bill is her nephew. _____

3. Bill is her husband. _____

4. Bill is his father. _____

5. Bill is her father. _____

6. Bill is their uncle. _____

7. Bill is his nephew. _____

8. Bill is their grandson. _____

9. Bill is her cousin. _____

10. Bill is his wife's brother. _____

3 A Read and answer.

1. Bill has two aunts. *Their* names are Grace and Nina.
2. Bill has one uncle. ___His___ name is Ron.
3. Bill's children have two cousins. ___Their___ names are Steve and Laura.
4. Bill has one niece. ___Her___ name is Laura.
5. Bill's sister and her husband have two children. ___Their___ names are Steve and Laura.
6. Bill and his wife have two daughters. ___Their___ names are Carla and Emma.
7. Bill's father has parents. ___Their___ names are George and Ida.
8. Bill's grandparents have one granddaughter. ___Her___ name is Ann.
9. Ann has one nephew. ___His___ name is John.
10. Carla, Emma, and John have three uncles. ___Their___ names are Louis, Eric, and Pablo.

3 B Class Activity. Give your book to a classmate.

Teacher: Who has your book?

Student 1: _____ has my book.

Teacher: Who has Juan's book?

Student 2: ___He___ has his book.

Optional Activity. With a partner, show a photograph of your family. Talk about it.

To have 47

LESSON 4

Who is . . .?, Who are . . .?

1 A   Read and write.

1. Our uncle has a son. Who is he? — *He is your cousin.*

2. Our father has two sisters. Who are they? — *They are your aunts.*
3. Our aunt has two children. Who are they? — *They are your cousin.*
4. Our sister has a daughter. Who is she? — *She is your niece.*
5. Our father has a brother. Who is he? — *He is your uncle.*
6. Our brother has a son. Who is he? — *He is your nephew.*
7. Who is our mother's father? — *grandfather.*
8. Who are our son's sisters? — *daughters*
9. Who are our father's parents? — *grandmother and grandfather*
10. Who is our mother's husband? — *father.*
11. Who is our uncle's wife? — *aunt.*

48   Chapter 3

1 B Read and answer.

1. Is my father's brother my cousin? _No, he isn't._
2. Is my mother's sister my aunt? _Yes, she is._
3. Are my uncle's children my cousins? _Yes, they're._
4. Are my brother's sons my uncles? _No, he isn't._
5. Is my mother's father my grandfather? _Yes, he is._
6. Are my sister's daughters my nieces? _Yes, they're._
7. Are my father's parents my grandparents? _Yes, they're._
8. Is my grandmother's husband my grandfather? _Yes, he is._
9. Is my sister's son my nephew? _Yes, he is._
10. Are my aunt's sons my brothers? _No, They aren't._

1 C Listen and answer.

1 D Read and write.

1. Our uncles and aunts don't have children.
   We don't have cousins.

2. His brothers and sisters don't have daughters.
   He doesn't have niece.

3. Her father and mother don't have brothers.
   She doesn't have uncles.

4. Their grandparents don't have daughters.
   They don't have aunts.

5. Our brothers and sisters don't have sons.
   We don't have nephew.

6. My father and mother don't have sisters.
   I don't have aunts.

2 A Listen and put in 11 carets. (∧)

Our uncle's wife ∧[has] a Japanese father and a French mother. Uncle ∧[is] half Spanish and half British. He and his wife ∧[have] six children. Daughters ∧[Their] French and Japanese names, and ∧[their] sons ∧[have] Spanish and British names. The children's grandparents ∧[are] from four countries, but ∧[their] grandchildren ∧[are] 100 percent American.

2 B Write these words above the carets.

are   are   has   have   have   have   is   our   their   their   their

3 A Listen to the commands.

1. Point to your nose.
2. Point to your left arm.
3. Point to your eyes.
4. Point to your toes.
5. Point to your right leg.
6. Point to your left ear.
7. Point to your mouth.
8. Point to your chin.
9. Point to your neck.
10. Point to your cheeks.
11. Point to your teeth.
12. Point to your fingers on your left hand.

3 B Class Activity. Stand in groups of 3 and give commands.

1. Point to her head.
2. Point to his right foot.
3. Point to my right foot.
4. Point to your right foot.
5. Point to my right ear.
6. Point to his left arm.
7. Point to your left leg.
8. Point to his right leg.
9. Point to my toes.
10. Point to her eyes.

4 A Find these words. Circle.

GRANDMOTHER	PARENTS	UNCLE	AUNT
FATHER	MOTHER	BROTHER	SISTER
WIFE	HUSBAND	SON	DAUGHTER
CHILDREN	NEPHEW	NIECE	COUSIN

```
G A Z T V P F D U B V F P N
H R N G P S A F N R B I X I
D U A V T U O O U O Z W U S
A R M N H E O N E T P C N W
N N E H D S H C M H A C C E
W P T P Q M E P J E R H L Y
H I H M T I O U E R E I E M
U S F B N A Q T E N N L C O
S Z S E Q Z F C H O T D G T
B R B C O U S I N E S R H H
A E A F A T H E R I R E I E
N Q N P N E P H E W Z N P R
D O D B D A U G H T E R C M
S I S T E R A B K T K R Q Z
```

4 B With a partner, put the words you found in alphabetical order.

aunt	Parents
Son	Mother
Father	cousin
Nephew	wife
Sister	Brothers
Daughter	Niece
grandmother	uncle
Husband	children

4 Present tenses
Going-to future

LESSON 1
simple present

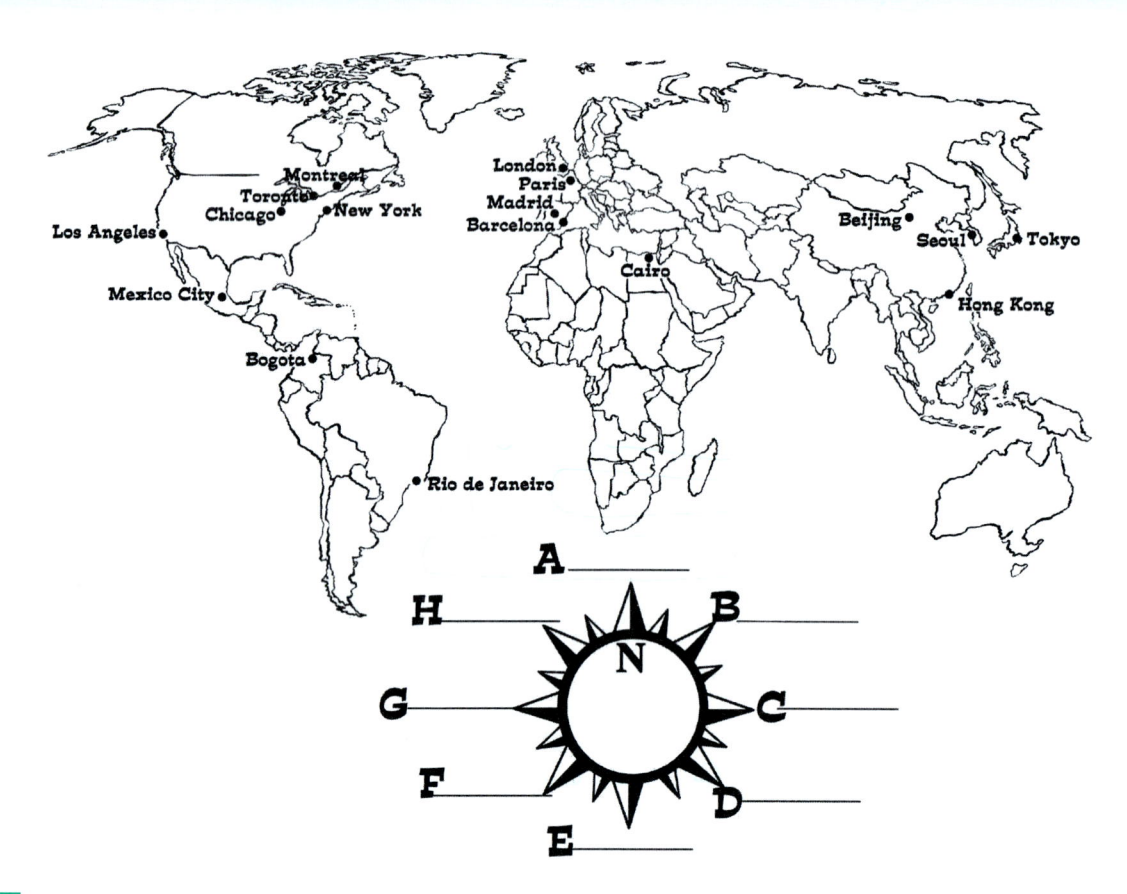

1 A Listen.

1 B Spelling. Write the words on the blanks.

1 C Class Activity. Face north and listen to the commands.

52   Chapter 4

1 D Read and answer.

1. From Chicago to New York, do we go east? — Yes
2. From New York to Toronto, do we go northeast? — No
3. From Beijing to Seoul, do we go north? — _____
4. From Paris to Cairo, do we go southwest? — _____
5. From Los Angeles to Tokyo, do we go west? — _____
6. From Rio de Janeiro to Mexico City, do we go northwest? — _____
7. From Paris to Barcelona, do we go north? — _____
8. From Seoul to Los Angeles, do we go east? — _____
9. From Chicago to Mexico City, do we go southwest? — _____
10. From Montreal to New York, do we go south? — _____
11. From Bogota to Rio de Janeiro, do we go northeast? — _____
12. From Madrid to London, do we go west? — _____

GRAMMAR FOCUS

From Chicago to New York, **I go** east.
From Chicago to New York, **you go** east.
From Chicago to New York, **he goes** east.
From Chicago to New York, **she goes** east.
From Chicago to New York, **we go** east.
From Chicago to New York, **they go** east.

2 Read and write.

1. We are in Chicago. (east / west)
   _____ We go east _____ to get to New York.

2. Bill is in Paris. (southeast / southwest)
   _____ He goes _____ to get to Spain.

3. We are in Toronto. (southeast / southwest)
   _____ to get to Chicago.

4. We are in Japan. (east / west)
   _____ to get to China.

5. Bill and his son are in Mexico. (southeast / southwest)
   _____ to get to Brazil.

6. Bill's mother is in Los Angeles. (north / south)
   _____ to get to San Francisco.

7. I am in Madrid. (northeast / northwest)
   _____ to get to Paris.

8. Bill's daughters are in New York. (northeast / northwest)
   _____ to get to Toronto.

9. We are in Korea. (east / west)
   _____ to get to Canada.

10. We are in Cairo. (northeast / northwest)
    _____ to get to Madrid.

11. We are in London. (east / west)
    _____ to get to Paris.

12. Bill's wife is in Rio de Janeiro. (northwest / northeast)
    _____ to get to Bogota.

Chapter 4

3 A Listen.

A. _____

B. _____

C. _____

D. _____

E. _____

F. _____

G. _____

H. _____

I. _____

3 B Listen and write the letters.

1. _____
2. _____
3. _____
4. _____
5. _____ _____
6. _____ _____
7. _____ _____
8. _____ _____ _____
9. _____ _____ _____

3 C Spelling. Write the words on the blanks.

Present tenses, *going-to* future   55

LESSON 2

simple present
adjectives
all/some/any

1 A   Listen.

A. _____   B. _____

C. _____   D. _____   E. _____

F. _____   G. _____

1 B   Listen and write the letters.

1. ____   4. ____   7. ____ ____
2. ____   5. ____   8. ____ ____
3. ____   6. ____ ____   9. ____ ____ ____

1 C   Spelling. Write the words on the blanks.

56   Chapter 4

2 A Read and answer.

1. Do you eat when you are hungry? _____Yes_____
2. Do you sleep when you are tired? _____
3. Do you cry when you are happy? _____
4. Do you wash when you are clean? _____
5. Do you run when you are tired? _____
6. Do you drink when you are thirsty? _____
7. Do you wash when you are dirty? _____
8. Do you eat when you are thirsty? _____
9. Do you cry when you are sad? _____
10. Do you wash your hands when your fingers are dirty? _____

GRAMMAR FOCUS

He **eats**.	He **washes**.	He **cries**.
(eat + s)	(wash + es)	(cry − y + ies)

2 B Read and answer.

1. What do children do when they are hungry? _____They eat._____
2. What do we do when we are tired? _____
3. What does Bill's wife do when she is thirsty? _____
4. What does Bill's son do when he is dirty? _____
5. What do Bill's daughters do when they are sad? _____
6. What does the dog do when it is hungry? _____
7. What do you and your brother do when you are thirsty? _____
8. What do you do when you are dirty? _____
9. What do children do when they are sad? _____
10. What does Bill's mother do when she is tired? _____

Present tenses, *going-to* future

3 A Listen.

A. _____

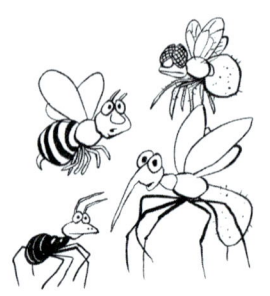

B. _____

C. _____

D. _____

E. _____

F. _____

3 B Listen and write the letters.

1. _____
2. _____
3. _____ _____
4. _____ _____
5. _____ _____ _____
6. _____ _____ _____

3 C Spelling. Write the words on the blanks.

GRAMMAR FOCUS

All

Some

58   Chapter 4

4 A Read and answer.

1. Do all insects eat? _Yes_
2. Do some animals swim? _____
3. Do all people sleep? _____
4. Do all animals run? _____
5. Do some animals fly? _____
6. Do some people swim? _____
7. Do all people eat and drink? _____
8. Do some animals drive? _____
9. Do all insects run and swim? _____
10. Do all animals cry? _____

4 B Read and answer.

1. Are there some insects that drive?
   No, there aren't any.
2. Are there some animals that don't run?
   Yes, there are some.
3. Are there some people that don't drive?
   _____
4. Are there some insects that cry?
   _____
5. Are there some people who don't sleep?
   _____
6. Are there some animals that fly?
   _____
7. Are there some people who don't eat and drink?
   _____
8. Are there some animals that don't swim?
   _____
9. Are there some animals that don't have teeth?
   _____
10. Are there some animals that swim and fly?
    _____

Present tenses, *going-to* future

LESSON 3

present continuous
and, or, but

1 A   Listen.

1 B   Listen and write the letters.

1. _____
2. _____
3. _____
4. _____

5. _____ _____
6. _____ _____
7. _____ _____
8. _____ _____

9. _____ _____ _____
10. _____ _____ _____
11. _____ _____ _____
12. _____ _____ _____ _____

1 C   Spelling. Write the words on the blanks below.

A. _____
B. _____
C. _____

D. _____
E. _____
F. _____

G. _____
H. _____
I. _____

J. _____
K. _____
L. _____

60   Chapter 4

1 D Read and answer.

1. Is Fernando wearing pants? _Yes_
2. Is Rosa wearing a jacket? _____
3. Are Fernando and Rosa wearing belts? _____
4. Is Fernando wearing a suit? _____
5. Is Rosa wearing a necktie? _____
6. Is Rosa wearing sandals? _____
7. Are Fernando and Rosa wearing clothes? _____
8. Is Rosa wearing a dress? _____
9. Is Fernando wearing a jacket? _____
10. Are Fernando and Rosa wearing glasses? _____

2 A Look at the back cover and listen to the colors.

2 B Make a chart. Tell what colors you are wearing.

	red	blue	black	green	yellow	white	brown	orange	pink	gray	tan	purple
Juan	X		X			X						
Maria		X				X					X	

2 C With a partner, write sentences about your classmates.

Juan is wearing red, black, and white but not blue or tan.

Maria is wearing blue, white, and tan but not brown or orange.

Optional Activity. Write five sentences about yourself.

I'm wearing blue and green but not orange and white.

Present tenses, *going-to* future

3 A   Listen.

A.  _____   B.  _____   C. _____

D.  _____   E.  _____   F. _____

G.  _____   H.  _____   I. _____

3 B   Spelling. Write the words on the blanks.

3 C   Class Activity. Listen and follow the directions.

62   Chapter 4

4 A Read and answer.

1. Are you waving? _No_
2. Are you sitting? _____
3. Are you clapping? _____
4. Are you reading? _____
5. Are you swimming? _____
6. Are you writing? _____
7. Are you standing? _____
8. Are you listening? _____
9. Are you eating? _____
10. Are you thinking? _____

GRAMMAR FOCUS

drink + ing = drink**ing**
eat + ing = eat**ing**
sleep + ing = sleep**ing**
wav~~e~~ + ing = wav**ing**

writ~~e~~ + ing = writ**ing**
sit + t + ing = si**tt**ing
run + n + ing = run**n**ing
swim + m + ing = swim**m**ing

4 B Look at the pictures and answer.

1. Is Keiko waving or clapping? _She's waving._
2. Is Keiko standing or sitting? _____ 
3. Is Keiko reading or writing? _____ 
4. Is Keiko running or swimming? _____ 
5. Is Keiko eating or drinking? _____ 
6. Is Keiko driving or flying? _____ 

Present tenses, *going-to* future

LESSON 4
going-to future

1 A   Listen.

A. They're playing _____.

B. They're playing _____.

C. They're playing _____.

D. They're playing _____.

E. They're playing _____.

F. They're playing _____.

1 B   Listen and write the letters.

1. ____
2. ____
3. ____
4. ____

5. ____ ____
6. ____ ____
7. ____ ____ ____
8. ____ ____ ____

1 C   Spelling. Write the words on the blanks.

64   Chapter 4

GRAMMAR FOCUS

Bill is **going to** play tennis.   Bill is **playing** tennis.

2 A Listen.

A   B   C   D

E   F   G   H

I   J   K   L

2 B Read and answer.

1. Bill is playing soccer.   _F_
2. Bill is going to play tennis.   ____
3. Bill is going to play soccer.   ____
4. Bill is playing volleyball.   ____
5. Bill is playing basketball.   ____
6. Bill is going to play golf.   ____

7. Bill is going to play volleyball.   ____
8. Bill is going to play baseball.   ____
9. Bill is playing tennis.   ____
10. Bill is playing golf.   ____
11. Bill is going to play basketball.   ____
12. Bill is playing baseball.   ____

Present tenses, *going-to* future   **65**

3 Read and write.

1. I am listening now.
   I am going to listen tomorrow.

2. He is swimming now.
   _____

3. We are eating now.
   _____

4. She is crying now.
   _____

5. They are standing now.
   _____

6. Are you driving now?
   _____

7. I am not listening now.
   _____

8. We aren't sitting now.
   _____

9. Is she sleeping now?
   _____

4 A Listen and put in 15 carets (^).

Miguel: My sister going to go to Hawaii.
Rosa: Hawaii? How wonderful! When is she going go?
Miguel: Tomorrow. She's going to be Hawaii two weeks. She's going to and golf every day.
Rosa: You going to go to Hawaii?
Miguel: No, I'm to go to Chicago. It's January and going to go to a cold city.
Rosa: Don't sad. Chicago is wonderful city.
Miguel: Not January. I am going to wear a jacket and gloves Chicago and my is going to wear sandals a T-shirt in Hawaii.

4 B Write these words above the carets.

a   and   are   be   for   going   I'm   in   in   is   play   sister   swim   to

66   Chapter 4

5 A Find these words. Circle.

- GO
- WASH
- DRIVE
- CLAP
- POINT
- EAT
- FLY
- CRY
- STAND
- LISTEN
- DRINK
- SWIM
- WEAR
- SIT
- THINK
- SLEEP
- RUN
- WAVE
- WRITE
- READ

```
E E K O J X R S E W G W R T F
S T A N D F O P A W U T E L A
Q Y S L E E P C B R J H I A P
Q V X O C L H H K I A I C M R
G S B L K C B N P T W N A D L
O I I C K I T O E A K J G E
E T Q B C R W H I L V R E A D
I A O H D N F V N A E V T Z N
R W T C T B U J T E C F K E O
S T Q P W A S H U F R M T Q G
N Q F S W R A R T E Y S S B F
G C L A P X E J V X I W R U N
Z C N T T D M I U L I F F C R
S W I M M W R D Z N V N F L Y
G K V T U D U O H K X V X L G
```

5 B With a partner, write the words you found in alphabetical order.

clap   fly   run   think

___   ___   ___   ___

___   ___   ___   ___

___   ___   ___   ___

___   ___   ___   ___

Present tenses, *going-to* future **67**

5 Future with *will*

LESSON 1

will

1 A   Listen.

A. 2:00
B. 7:00
C. 4:10
D. 1:15
E. 5:20
F. 12:30
G. 10:40
H. 8:45
I. 12:00
J. 12:00

1 B   Listen and write the letters.

1. ____
2. ____
3. ____
4. ____ ____
5. ____ ____
6. ____ ____
7. ____ ____ ____
8. ____ ____ ____
9. ____ ____ ____

68   Chapter 5

GRAMMAR FOCUS

It is 3 o'clock. In one hour, it **is going to be** 4 o'clock.= In one hour, it **will be** 4 o'clock.

2 A Read and answer.

1. It is 3:00. Will it be 4:00 in one hour? _Yes_
2. It is 10:00. Will it be 11:00 in one hour? _____
3. It is 6:00. Will it be 9:00 in two hours? _____
4. It is 2:00. Will it be 5:00 in three hours? _____
5. It is 7:00. Will it be noon in four hours? _____
6. It is 8:00. Will it be 9:30 in one and a half hours? _____
7. It is 1:30. Will it be 3:00 in two and a half hours? _____
8. It is midnight. Will it be 12:30 in one and a half hours? _____
9. It is 9:00. Will it be 11:00 in three hours? _____
10. It is midnight. Will it be noon in twelve hours? _____

2 B Listen and answer.

2 C Read and answer.

1. It is 3:00. What time will it be in one hour?
   It will be 4:00.
2. It is 6:00. What time will it be in one hour?
   _____
3. It is 10:00. What time will it be in one and a half hours?
   _____
4. It is 5:30. What time will it be in two hours?
   _____
5. It is noon. What time will it be in a half hour?
   _____
6. It is midnight. What time will it be in twelve hours?
   _____
7. It is 4:45. What time will it be in one hour?
   _____
8. It is 8:30. What time will it be in a half hour?
   _____

Future with *will*

3 A Listen.

A. _____

B. _____
breakfast.

C. _____

D. _____
his teeth.

E. _____

F. _____

G. _____
his house.

H. _____
at the airport.

I. _____

J. _____
the airplane.

K. _____

3 B Listen and write the letters.

1. ____
2. ____
3. ____ ____
4. ____ ____
5. ____ ____
6. ____ ____ ____
7. ____ ____ ____

3 C Spelling. Write the words on the blanks.

70   Chapter 5

4 A Read and answer.

1. Will Bill eat breakfast after he gets up?   _Yes._
2. Will Bill get dressed before he shaves?   _____
3. Will Bill brush his teeth before he showers?   _____
4. Will Bill leave his house after he gets dressed? _____
5. Will Bill leave his house before 9:30?   _____
6. Will Bill check in before he arrives at the airport? _____
7. Will Bill board the plane after he checks in?   _____
8. Will Bill's plane take off before he boards it?   _____
9. Will the plane take off after 12:00 noon?   _____

4 B Listen and answer.

4 C Class Activity. Make a chart.

Today _Monday_   Tomorrow _Tuesday_

	get up	breakfast	lunch	dinner	go to bed
Juan	7:30	8:15	12:00	6:00	10:30
Maria	6:00	7:30	12:30	6:00	9:45

4 D With a partner, write five sentences.

Juan will eat lunch at 12:00 tomorrow.
Maria will eat dinner at 6:00.
_____
_____
_____
_____
_____

Future with *will*

LESSON 2

ordinal numbers
comes before/follows

1 A Listen.

1 B Spelling. Write each month.

1 C Read and answer.

1. Does June come before July? _____
2. Does September follow August? _____
3. Does February come before January? _____
4. Does March follow April? _____
5. Does May follow June? _____

GRAMMAR FOCUS

Monday **comes before** Tuesday.
Tuesday **follows** Monday.

6. Does October come before November? _____
7. Does March come before February? _____
8. Do October and November follow September? _____
9. Do January and February follow March? _____
10. Do April and May come before June? _____

1 D Listen and write.

Future with *will* 73

GRAMMAR FOCUS

first   second   third   fourth

2 A Look at the calendar on pages 72 and 73 and listen.

January is the first month.
February is the second month.
March is the third month.
April is the fourth month.
May is the fifth month.
June is the sixth month.

July is the seventh month.
August is the eighth month.
September is the ninth month.
October is the tenth month.
November is the eleventh month.
December is the twelfth month.

2 B Read and answer.

1. What's the second month?   *February*
2. What's the fourth month?   _____
3. What's the first month?   _____
4. What's the sixth month?   _____
5. What's the tenth month?   _____
6. What's the third month?   _____
7. What are the fifth and sixth months?   _____

8. What are the eleventh and twelfth months?   _____

9. What are the seventh and eighth months?   _____

10. What are the ninth, tenth, and eleventh months?   _____

Chapter 5

2 C Listen and answer.

3 A Listen.

A.  _____ B.  _____ C.  _____ D. _____

E.  _____ F.  _____ G.  _____ H. _____

3 B Listen and write the letters.

1. ____
2. ____
3. ____
4. ____

5. ____ ____
6. ____ ____
7. ____ ____
8. ____ ____ ____

3 C Spelling. Write the words on the blanks.

Future with *will* 75

LESSON 3

will not, won't

GRAMMAR FOCUS	
I **will not** go.	I **won't** go.
He **will not** go.	He **won't** go.
They **will not** go.	They **won't** go.

1 A Look at the calendar for 2050, read, and answer.

1. New Year's Day is the first of January. Will it be on Saturday in 2050?
   Yes, it will.

2. Lincoln's Birthday is the twelfth of February. Will it be on Friday in 2050?
   No, it won't.

3. In the United States, Mother's Day is the second Sunday in May. Will it be on the 8th of May in 2050?

4. Christmas is the 25th of December. Will in be on Sunday in 2050?

5. In the United States, Memorial Day is the last Monday in May. Will it be on the 29th of May in 2050?

6. In Canada, Thanksgiving is the second Monday in October. Will it be on the 17th of October in 2050?

7. In Mexico, Labor Day is the first of May. Will it be on Saturday in 2050?

76   Chapter 5

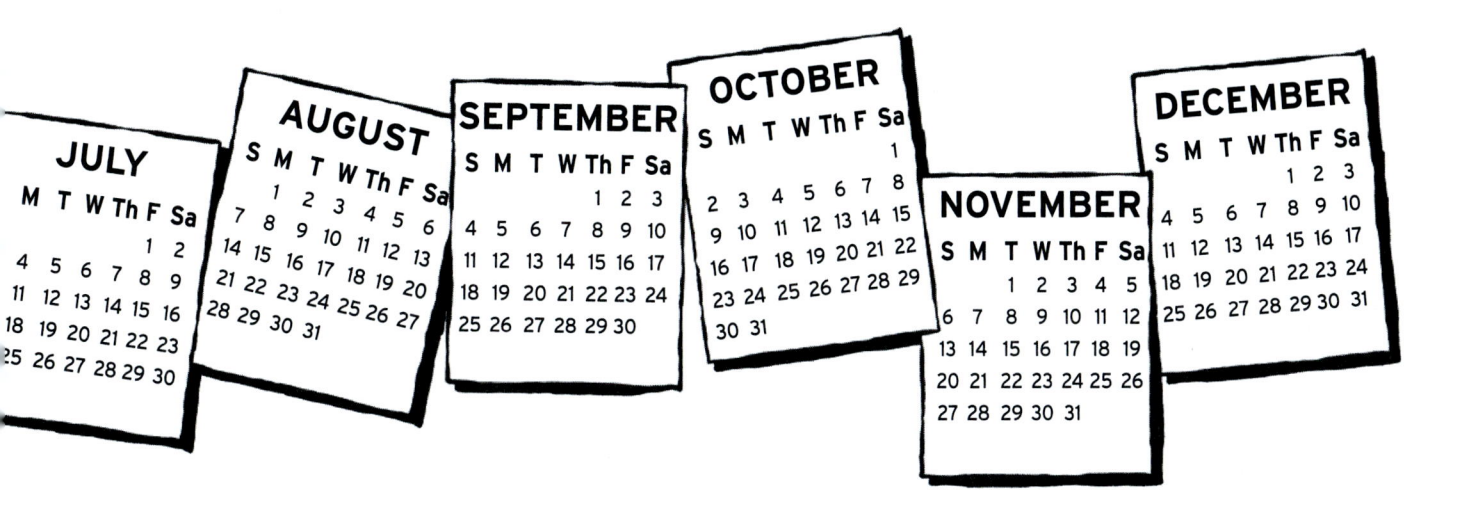

8. In the United States, Father's Day is the third Sunday in June. Will it be on the 19th of June in 2050?

   _____

9. In Japan, Thanksgiving Day is November 23rd. Will it be on Wednesday in 2050?

   _____

10. In the United States, Labor Day is the first Monday in September. Will it be on the 5th of September in 2050?

    _____

11. In France, Mother's Day is the last Sunday in May. Will it be on the 31st of May in 2050?

    _____

12. In the United States, Thanksgiving Day is the fourth Thursday in November. Will it be on the 24th of November in 2050?

    _____

1 B Class Activity. Make a chart.

Juan says, "My birthday will be on the second Monday in June in 2050."

name	birthday
Juan	June 13th

Future with *will*   77

GRAMMAR FOCUS

I will = I'll	My brother will = My brother'll	It will = It'll
You will = You'll	She will = she'll	We will = We'll
He will = He'll	Rosa will = Rosa'll	They will = They'll

2 A Read and answer.

1. Tomorrow we'll go to Paris. — *No*
2. Tomorrow we'll eat breakfast at noon. — _____
3. Tomorrow we'll read our English book. — _____
4. Tomorrow we'll wash our hands. — _____
5. Tomorrow we'll stand up and sit down. — _____
6. Tomorrow Bill's son'll eat insects. — _____
7. Tomorrow Bill's grandmother will swim to Spain. — _____
8. Tomorrow we'll wear orange shoes. — _____

2 B Read and write.

1. I'm 20 years old. (ten years)
   In ten years I'll be 30 years old.
2. My brother is 11 years old. (six years)
   In six years he'll be 17 years old.
3. My sister's 12 years old. (eight years)
   _____
4. My father and mother are 35 years old. (fifteen years)
   _____
5. You're 15 years old. (five years)
   _____
6. I'm 16 years old. (twenty years)
   _____
7. We're 20 years old. (nine years)
   _____
8. My nephew is 1 year old. (thirteen years)
   _____
9. Our aunt is 50. (twenty-five years)
   _____
10. Her cousins are 14. (twelve months)
    _____

Chapter 5

3 A Listen and put in 16 carets (∧).

Someday I will be rich! First, buy mother and father a new house. Second, give my sister the money need to go to university. Someday be a doctor and parents be very happy. Third, wife and will fly around the world. Fly to Paris, Madrid, Cairo, Bangkok, Hong Kong, Tokyo, San Francisco. Finally, buy a house California and have a big family.

3 B Write these words above the carets.

all   and   I   I'll   I'll   in   my   my   my   she'll   she'll   the   we'll   we'll   we'll   will

4 Find these words. Circle.

JANUARY	FEBRUARY	MARCH	APRIL
MAY	JUNE	JULY	AUGUST
SEPTEMBER	OCTOBER	NOVEMBER	DECEMBER

```
N A P R I L M Y H S D Y F O
W O F Y B P R N M E E G Y U
X H V W E A S A O P C O C G
I I R E U Y U X T T E I P P
B L R R M G K R O E M I N J
T M B G U B J B C M B B V N
O E A T P R E T A B E A E B
F S T R N M I R B E R Q T Q
J U L Y C H A P A R J U N E
A N C K D H Y Y S U O S T K
Z O Y S L C S U K Z G R H A
O C T O B E R K X G V U C G
R Z T H E B B B U U X M D S A
J A N U A R Y A W W I B I T
```

Future with *will*   79

6 Review

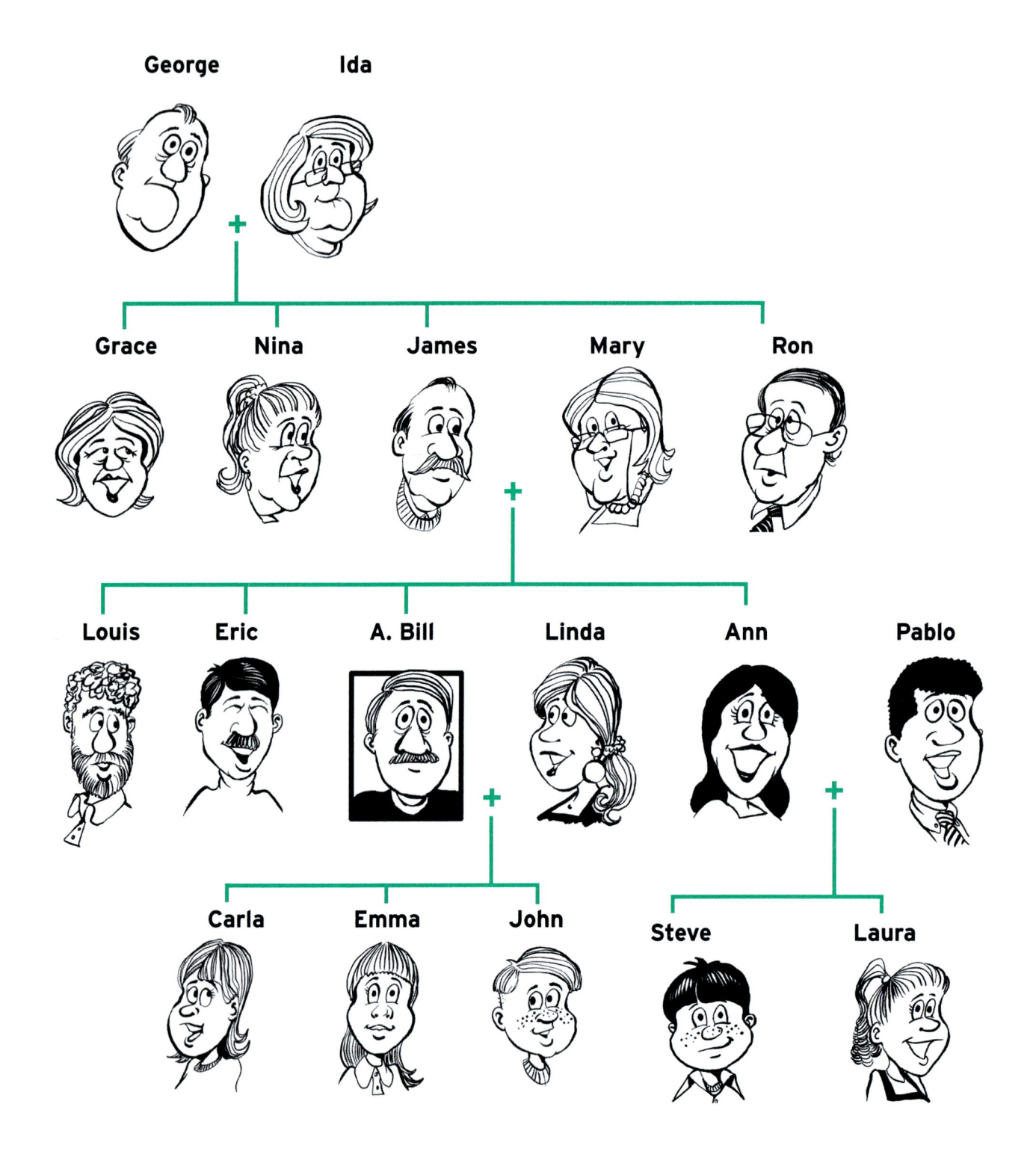

George **Ida**

Grace **Nina** **James** **Mary** **Ron**

Louis **Eric** **A. Bill** **Linda** **Ann** **Pablo**

Carla **Emma** **John** **Steve** **Laura**

1 Look at the family. Read and answer.

1. I have two sisters and one aunt. Who am I? _John_
2. My brothers and I have one sister. Who are we? _____
3. My mother has three sons. Who is she? _____
4. We have five grandchildren. Who are we? _____
5. My grandfather has four grandchildren. Who is he? _____
6. We have one brother and two cousins. Who are we? _____
7. My father has two sisters. Who are they? _____
8. My mother has three sons and one daughter. Who is she? _____
9. I have three brothers and two children. Who am I? _____
10. My nephew has three children. Who is he? _____

2 Look at the timeline. Answer.

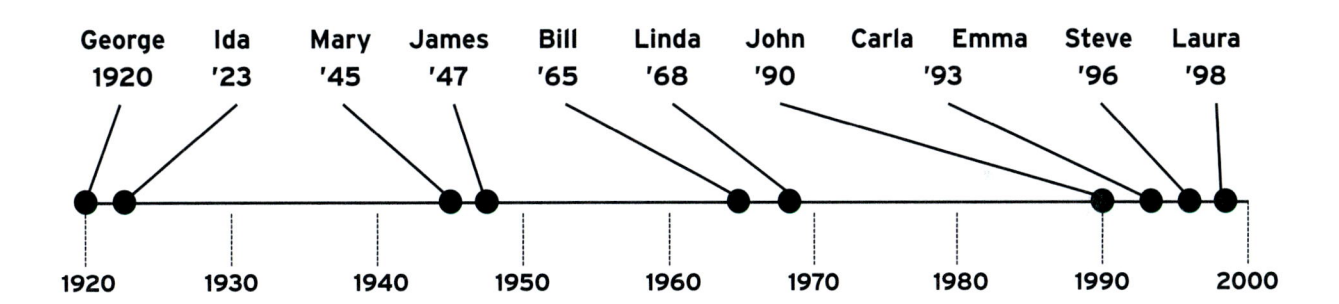

George	Ida	Mary	James	Bill	Linda	John	Carla	Emma	Steve	Laura
1920	'23	'45	'47	'65	'68	'90	'93	'96	'96	'98

1920 — 1930 — 1940 — 1950 — 1960 — 1970 — 1980 — 1990 — 2000

1. Will Bill be fifty-five in 2020? _Yes_
2. Will his wife be fifty-two in 2030? _____
3. Will his grandmother be 87 in 2020? _____
4. Will his niece be twelve in 2020? _____
5. Will his daughters be twenty in 2023? _____
6. Will his grandfather be eighty-one in 2021? _____
7. Will his son be thirty in 2020? _____
8. Will his mother be 75 in 2020? _____
9. Will his nephew be forty in 2036? _____
10. Will his father be sixty-five in 2025? _____

3 Read and answer.

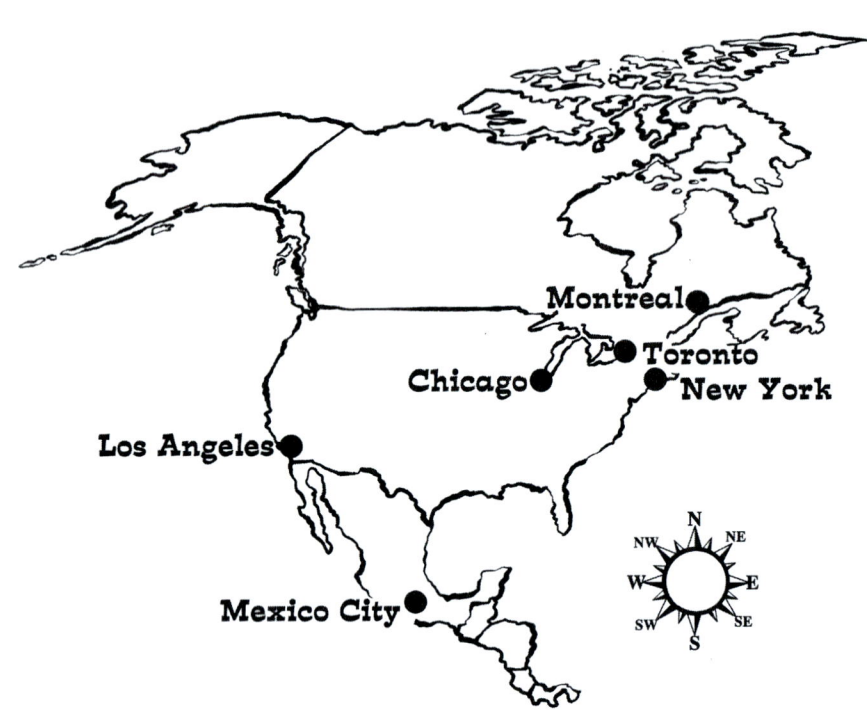

1. Joe is in Chicago.
   When he goes to New York, he goes east. _True_

2. Leah is in Los Angeles.
   When she goes to Chicago, she goes west. _____

3. My cousins are in Toronto.
   When they go to Los Angeles, they go southwest. _____

4. I am in Montreal.
   When I go to New York, I go northwest. _____

5. Roland is in Los Angeles.
   When he goes to Mexico City, he goes southeast. _____

6. My wife and I are in Chicago.
   When we go to Toronto, we go northeast. _____

4 Write.

1. Bill / New York / Chicago
   When Bill goes from New York to Chicago, he goes west.

2. I / New York / Montreal
   _____

3. My wife / Chicago / Mexico City.
   _____

82 Chapter 6

4. Carlos and Teresa / Mexico City / New York

_____

5. We / Toronto / Los Angeles

_____

6. Our son / Chicago / Montreal

_____

5 A Listen and put in 20 carets (ʌ).

Rita: Isabel, what you doing?

Isabel: Writing to my daughter.

Rita: Your daughter Colombia?

Isabel: No, daughter in Canada.

Rita: Oh, you a daughter in Canada?

Isabel: Yes, there a photograph of her the wall.

Rita: But there are photos. Is on the or on the left?

Isabel: On the left. Wearing a jacket and gloves.

Rita: Are the in the photo on the right?

Isabel: They are my and nephew.

Rita: Wearing sunglasses and sandals and they are very.

Isabel: Yes, they're in Mexico my parents. They go Mexico in January and because it cold.

5 B Write these words above the carets.

| are | children | February | happy | have | I'm | in | is | isn't | my |
| niece | on | right | she | she's | they're | to | two | who | with |

7 Can, cannot, can't
Know how to
Be able to

LESSON 1

can, cannot

1 A Listen.

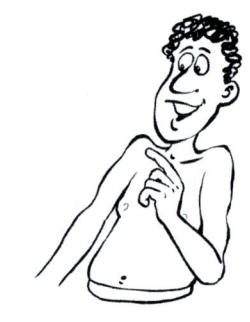

A.  _____ B.  _____ C.  _____ D. _____

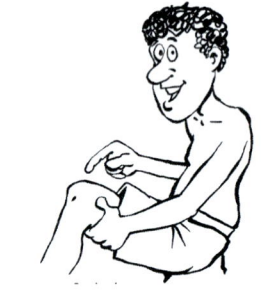

E. 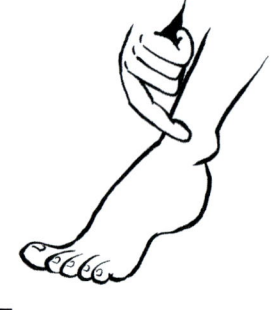 _____ F.  _____ G.  _____ H. _____

1 B Listen and write the letters.

1. ____
2. ____
3. ____
4. ____
5. ____ ____
6. ____ ____
7. ____ ____
8. ____ ____ ____
9. ____ ____ ____

1 C Spelling. Write the words on the blanks.

84 Chapter 7

2 Read and write.

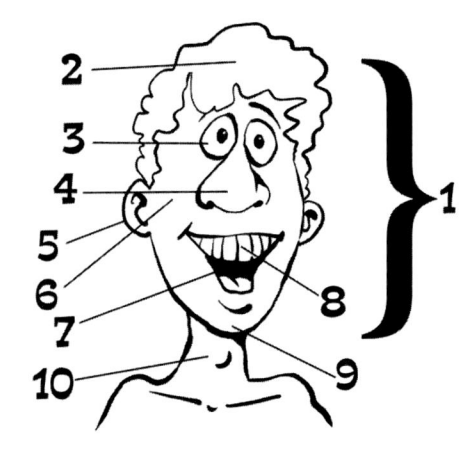

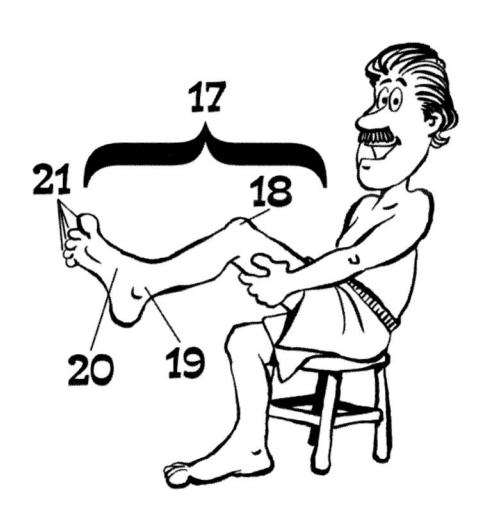

1. _head_ ———————— ankle
2. ———————————— arm
3. ———————————— cheek
4. ———————————— chin
5. ———————————— ear
6. ———————————— elbow
7. ———————————— eye
8. ———————————— fingers
9. ———————————— foot
10. ———————————— hair
11. ———————————— hand
12. ———————————— ~~head~~
13. ———————————— knee
14. ———————————— leg
15. ———————————— mouth
16. ———————————— neck
17. ———————————— nose
18. ———————————— shoulder
19. ———————————— teeth
20. ———————————— toes
21. ———————————— wrist

Can, cannot, can't
Know how to
Be able to

3 A Listen and do each action.

1. Touch your right ear with your left hand.
2. Touch your left arm with your right elbow.
3. Put your right hand behind your head.
4. Put the fingers of your left hand on your right shoulder.
5. Point to your stomach.
6. Touch your left ankle with your right hand.
7. Put your left arm above your eyes.
8. Point to the toes on your left foot.
9. Put the fingers of your right hand in your hair.
10. Put your hands on your knees.

3 B Class Activity. With a partner, practice the commands of 3A.

> **GRAMMAR FOCUS**
>
> can + not = **cannot**

4 Read and circle.

1. Can you touch your left leg with your left hand?

   (Yes, I can.)   No, I cannot.

2. Can you touch your right shoulder with your right elbow?

   Yes, I can.   No, I cannot.

3. Can you put your left foot under your right foot?

   Yes, I can.   No, I cannot.

4. Can you point to your stomach?

   Yes, I can.   No, I cannot.

5. Can you put the fingers of your right hand on your right elbow?

   Yes, I can.   No, I cannot.

6. Can you put your right leg on your left ankle?

   Yes, I can.   No, I cannot.

7. Can you put your left arm in front of your face?

   Yes, I can.   No, I cannot.

8. Can you touch your nose with your toes?

   Yes, I can.   No, I cannot.

86   Chapter 7

5A Listen.

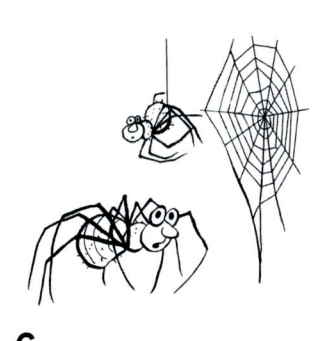

A._____ B._____ C._____ D._____

E._____ F._____ G._____ H._____

I._____ J._____ K._____ L._____

5B Listen and write the letters.

1. ____
2. ____
3. ____ ____
4. ____ ____ ____
5. ____ ____ ____
6. ____ ____ ____
7. ____ ____ ____
8. ____ ____ ____
9. ____ ____ ____

5C Spelling. Write the words on the blanks.

Can, cannot, can't
Know how to
Be able to

LESSON 2

can, can't
know how to

GRAMMAR FOCUS

cannot = **can't**

1 A Read and answer.

1. Can chickens swim? _No, they can't._
2. Can dogs run? _____
3. Can spiders fly? _____
4. Can horses play golf? _____
5. Can cats eat and drink? _____
6. Can snakes clap? _____
7. Can bees read and write? _____
8. Can fish and ducks swim? _____
9. Can dogs drive? _____
10. Can monkeys stand up and sit down? _____

1 B Listen and answer.

2 A Read and answer.

1. What can't a horse do?   eat / fly
   It can't fly.
2. What can't bees do?   drive / fly
   They can't drive.
3. What can't birds do?   read / eat
   _____
4. What can't a fish do?   swim / stand up
   _____
5. What can't a snake do?   clap / sleep
   _____
6. What can't sheep do?   drink / wave
   _____

88   Chapter 7

7. What can't monkeys do?   run / shave

_____

8. What can't a duck do?   read and write / fly and swim

_____

9. What can't a dog do?   brush its teeth / sit down

_____

10. What can't spiders do?   eat insects / eat pizza

_____

> **GRAMMAR FOCUS**
> one sheep   two sheep~~s~~
> one fish   two fish~~es~~

2 B Write sentences.

1. Chickens / run / swim
   Chickens can run but they can't swim.

2. dogs / fly / run
   Dogs can't fly but they can run.

3. bees / fly / swim
   _____

4. horses / play basketball / run
   _____

5. monkeys / sit down / drive
   _____

6. fish / swim / run
   _____

7. ducks / shave and shower / fly and swim
   _____

8. snakes / eat and drink / sit down
   _____

9. cats / sleep / read and write
   _____

10. monkeys / fly / clap
    _____

Can, cannot, can't
Know how to
Be able to

3 A Listen.

A.  _____ B.  _____ C. 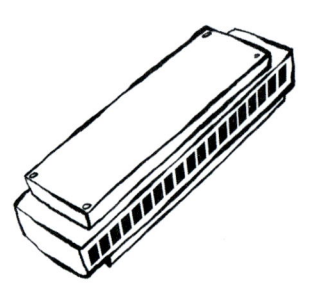 _____ D. _____

E.  _____ F.  _____ G.  _____ H. _____

3 B Listen and write the letters.

1. ____
2. ____
3. ____ ____
4. ____ ____

5. ____ ____
6. ____ ____
7. ____ ____ ____
8. ____ ____ ____

3 C Spelling. Write the words on the blanks.

90 Chapter 7

GRAMMAR FOCUS
I can drive. = I **know how to** drive.

4 Read and answer.

1. Do you know how to play the guitar? _____
2. Do you know how to play dominos? _____
3. Do you know how to play baseball? _____
4. Do you know how to play the piano? _____
5. Do you know how to play chess? _____
6. Do you know how to play the drums? _____
7. Do you know how to play soccer? _____
8. Do you know how to play checkers? _____
9. Do you know how to play Ping-Pong? _____
10. Do you know how to play the harmonica? _____

GRAMMAR FOCUS	
to play **the** piano	to play chess
to play **the** guitar	to play baseball

5 Class Activity. Make a chart. Tell what you know how to do.

	piano	chess	guitar	harmonica	checkers	drums	dominos	ping pong
Juan	No	Yes	Yes	No	No	No	Yes	Yes
Maria	Yes	No	Yes	No	Yes	No	No	Yes

Write five sentences about your classmates.

Juan can play dominos, but he doesn't know how to play checkers.
Maria can play the guitar, but she doesn't know how to play the harmonica.

_____
_____
_____
_____
_____

Can, cannot, can't
Know how to
Be able to

LESSON 3

be able to
because

1 A Listen.

A._____   B._____   C._____

D._____   E._____   F._____

G._____   H._____   I._____

1 B Listen and write the letters.

1. ____
2. ____
3. ____ ____
4. ____ ____

5. ____ ____
6. ____ ____ ____
7. ____ ____ ____
8. ____ ____ ____ ____

1 C Spelling. Write the words on the blanks.

92   Chapter 7

> **GRAMMAR FOCUS**
>
> can = **be able to**
> He can swim. = He **is able to** swim.

2 A Read and answer.

1. You need a racket to be able to play tennis. _True_
2. You need clubs to be able to play golf. _____
3. You need skates to be able to fish. _____
4. You need a bat to be able to play baseball. _____
5. You need a baseball to be able to play soccer. _____
6. You need an American football to be able to ski. _____
7. You need dominos to be able to play chess. _____
8. You need a soccer ball to be able to play soccer. _____
9. You need a paddle to be able to play Ping-Pong. _____
10. You need skates to be able to play hockey. _____

2 B Read and write.

1. What do we need to be able to play tennis? _We need rackets._
2. What do we need to be able to play basketball? _We need a basketball._
3. What do we need to be able to play soccer? _____
4. What do we need to be able to fish? _____
5. What do we need to be able to play hockey? _____
6. What do we need to be able to play Ping-Pong? _____
7. What do we need to be able to play baseball? _____
8. What do we need to be able to ski? _____
9. What do we need to be able to play volleyball? _____
10. What do we need to be able to play golf? _____

Can, cannot, can't
Know how to
Be able to

GRAMMAR FOCUS

Present	Future
can	will be able to
can't	won't be able to

3 A Listen.

1 2 3 4

5 6 7 8

GRAMMAR FOCUS

He is eating. He is hungry.
He is eating **because** he is hungry.

3 B Look at the pictures in 3A and complete the sentences.

1. They won't be able to fish _because they don't have fishing poles._
2. He won't be able to play tennis _____
3. She won't be able to play golf _____
4. He won't be able to play baseball _____
5. They won't be able to play soccer _____
6. They won't be able to play basketball _____
7. He won't be able to play hockey _____
8. They won't be able to play Ping-Pong _____

94 Chapter 7

4 A **Listen and put in 18 carets (∧).**

Jenny: Hi, Lydia, are you doing?

Lydia: Reading a book.

Jenny: You play tennis?

Lydia: No, I have my racket.

Jenny: Who has?

Lydia: Julie has and she and her mother be in Chicago today and tomorrow.

Jenny: You play tennis me tomorrow?

Lydia: No, I tomorrow but I will able play on Tuesday.

Jenny: No, you be able play tennis on Tuesday.

Lydia: Not?

Jenny: Because Julie going play tennis with me on Tuesday and she have your racket.

4 B **Write these words above the carets.**

be can can't don't I'm is it it to to to what why will will will with won't

Can, cannot, can't
Know how to
Be able to

8 Was, were
Had
Did

LESSON 1

was, were

1 A   Listen.

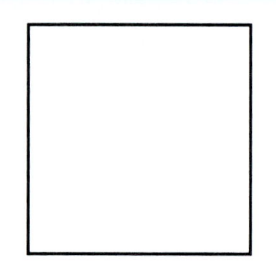

A. 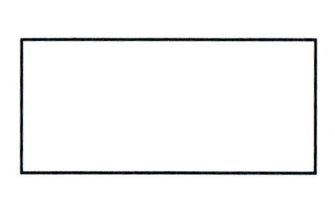 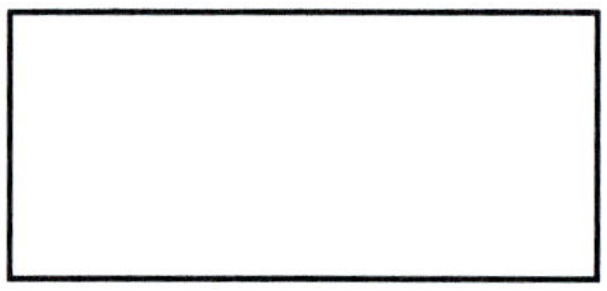 _____   B. 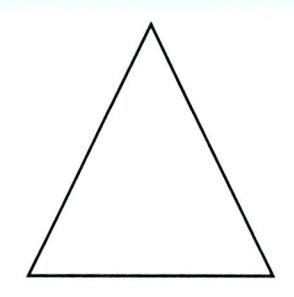 _____   C. 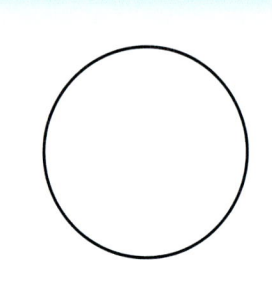 _____   D. _____

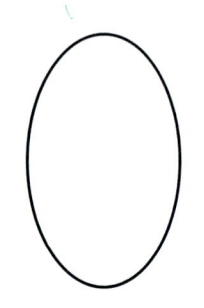

E. _____   F. _____   G. 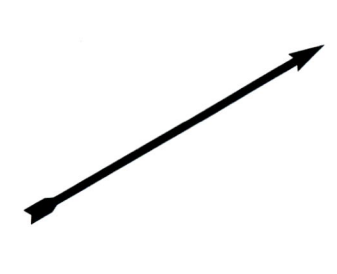 _____   H. _____

1 B   Listen and write the letters.

1. ____
2. ____
3. ____

4. ____
5. ____ ____
6. ____ ____

7. ____ ____
8. ____ ____ ____
9. ____ ____ ____

1 C   Spelling. Write the words on the blanks.

96   Chapter 8

2 A Follow the commands.

1. Draw a square on the board.
2. Draw a rectangle to the right of the square.
3. Draw a triangle to the left of the square.
4. Draw a circle in the square.
5. Draw an oval in the rectangle.
6. Draw two stars above the square.
7. Draw three lines under the rectangle.
8. Draw two arrows under the three lines.

GRAMMAR FOCUS

Present	Past
is	was
are	were

2 B Listen and answer.

2 C Erase the board. Read and answer.

1. Was the circle in the square? _Yes_
2. Was the rectangle to the right of the square? _____
3. Were the stars under the square? _____
4. Was the rectangle between the square and the triangle? _____
5. Was the oval in the rectangle? _____
6. Were the arrows above the lines? _____
7. Was the triangle next to the square? _____
8. Was the rectangle under the three lines? _____
9. Was the circle in the triangle? _____
10. Were the lines between the rectangle and the arrows? _____

Was, were
Had
Did

3 A Follow the directions.

3 B Read and answer.

1. Was there a book on the table? __Yes__
2. Were there two pencils to the right of the book? _____
3. Was there a half sheet of paper under the book? _____
4. Were there two sheets of paper on the book? _____
5. Was there a pencil to the left of the book? _____
6. Were there two sheets of paper under the book? _____
7. Was there a pencil on the book? _____
8. Were there two sheets of paper next to the book? _____
9. Was the book between two pencils? _____

3 C Listen and answer.

GRAMMAR FOCUS

Was not = was**n't**   Were not = were**n't**
The pencil was**n't** on the book.   The pens were**n't** on the book.

3 D Read and write.

was   wasn't   were   weren't

1. The book ____was____ on the table.
2. The pencils _____ in the book.
3. The half sheet of paper _____ to the left of the book.
4. The book _____ between the pencils.
5. The two sheets of paper _____ on the book.
6. There _____ a pencil to the right of the book.
7. There _____ a map above the book.
8. There _____ some paper clips under the book.

98   Chapter 8

LESSON 2
was, wasn't
had

1 A Listen.

A.  _____   B.  _____   C.  _____   D. _____

E.  _____   F.  _____   G.  _____   H. _____

1 B Listen and write the letters.

1. ____
2. ____
3. ____
4. ____ ____

5. ____ ____
6. ____ ____
7. ____ ____ ____
8. ____ ____ ____

1 C Spelling. Write the words on the lines.

Was, were
Had
Did

99

2. Look at the pictures. Read and answer.

1. Was Rosa at home at 7:00 yesterday?

   Yes, she was. She was at home.

2. Were they at school at 8:00?

   No, they weren't. They were at the mall.

3. Was she at the library at 5:30?

4. Were they at the gym at 3:00?

5. Were they at school at 9:00?

6. Was she at the supermarket at 1:30?

7. Was she at work at 5:30?

8. Were they at school at 10:30?

100   Chapter 8

3 A Class Activity. Make a chart. Tell where you were yesterday.

	school	work	super-market	mall	movies	library	gym
Juan	10:00–12:00	5:00–10:00					
Maria	8:00–3:00		3:30–4:15				
Paul	8:00–3:00					3:30–4:30	5:00–6:00

3 B With a partner, write five sentences about your classmates.

Juan wasn't at school yesterday from 5:00 to 10:00. He was at work. Maria and Paul weren't at work yesterday. They were at school from 8:00 to 3:00.

Was, were
Had
Did

4 A Listen.

A. _____

B. _____

C. _____

D. _____

E. _____

F. _____

G. _____

H. _____

I. _____

4 B Listen and write the letters.

1. ____
2. ____ ____
3. ____ ____
4. ____ ____
5. ____ ____
6. ____ ____ ____

4 C Spelling. Write the words on the blanks.

102   Chapter 8

5 A Read and answer.

1. The fisherman has a racket.   *False*
2. The basketball player has two basketballs.   _____
3. The baseball player has a ball and bat.   _____
4. The boxer has skates.   _____
5. The soccer player has a golf club.   _____
6. The volleyball player has three volleyballs.   _____
7. The hockey player has skates.   _____
8. The golfer has a golf club.   _____
9. The tennis player has a racket.   _____
10. The fisherman has a pole.   _____

5 B Listen and answer.

GRAMMAR FOCUS

Present
I **have** Juan's name.
Maria **has** Juan's name.

Past
I **had** Juan's name.
Maria **had** Juan's name.

6 A Class Activity.

Write your name on a piece of paper. Give it to a classmate. Answer questions.
    Teacher: Maria, whose name do you have?
    Maria: I have Juan's name.

Give the names to your teacher. Answer questions.
    Teacher: Maria, whose name did you have?
    Maria: I had Juan's name.

Was, were
Had
Did

LESSON 3
did, didn't

1 A Listen.

A.  _____ B.  _____ C.  _____ D. 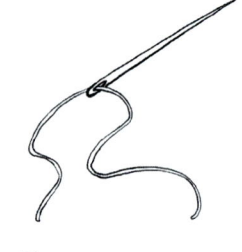 _____ E. _____

F.  _____ G.  _____ H.  _____ I.  _____ J. _____

1 B Listen and write the letters.

1. ____
2. ____
3. ____
4. ____ ____
5. ____ ____

6. ____ ____
7. ____ ____ ____
8. ____ ____ ____
9. ____ ____ ____
10. ____ ____ ____

1 C Spelling. Write the words on the blanks.

104 Chapter 8

2 A Listen.

A.  _____ B.  _____ C. _____

D.  _____ E.  _____ F.  _____ G. _____

H.  _____ I.  _____ J. _____

2 B Listen and write the letters.

1. ____
2. ____
3. ____
4. ____ ____
5. ____ ____

6. ____ ____
7. ____ ____ ____
8. ____ ____ ____
9. ____ ____ ____
10. ____ ____ ____

2 C Spelling. Write the words on the blanks.

Was, were
Had
Did

GRAMMAR FOCUS

Present	Past
do	did
does	
don't	didn't
doesn't	

3 Write the answers.

1. Did he sweep?
   No, he didn't because he didn't have a broom.

2. Did he shave?
   No,

3. Did she paint?
   No,

4. Did they sew?
   No,

5. Did he dig?
   No,

6. Did she write?
   No,

7. Did he drive?
   No,

8. Did we ride?
   No,

9. Did your grandmother sit?
   No,

4 A Listen and put in 25 carets (∧).

Our family lives Toronto but my parents are Mexico. In Mexico my father a teacher, and my mother a nurse. They rich, but they poor. Here in Canada father teaches Spanish, and mother works a library. There three children in our family. I'm 17 years old; my sister is; and my brother 10.

My father and mother happy when they in Mexico. But here Toronto my father has more money. Like Canada, but they like the weather. My father always says, "In Mexico it always warm."

My grandmother go with us to Canada. She happy to see our family go to Toronto. She wants us to return Mexico. Father and mother want to return, but my sister, my brother, and I want to return. We Canadians. Want to stay here.

4 B Write these words above the carets.

| 15 | are | are | didn't | don't | don't | from | in | in | in | is | my | my | my |
| they | to | was | was | was | wasn't | we | were | were | weren't | weren't |

Was, were
Had
Did

9 Simple past
Adjectives

LESSON 1

simple past

1 A Using a pencil, write the alphabet.

___ ___ ___ ___ ___ ___ ___ ___ ___
___ ___ ___ ___ ___ ___ ___ ___ ___
___ ___ ___ ___ ___ ___ ___ ___

1 B Using the alphabet, read and do the actions.

1. Circle the vowels. (a, e, i, o, u)
2. Underline the fourth letter.
3. Underline the sixth letter.
4. Underline the second letter.
5. Erase the seventh letter.
6. Erase the twenty-fifth letter.
7. Erase the third letter.
8. Mark out the letter before k.
9. Mark out the letter after s.
10. Mark out the last letter.

1 C Read and answer.

1. We circled a, e, i, o, and u.   _True_
2. We erased the sixth letter.   _____
3. We underlined the second letter.   _____
4. We marked out the last letter.   _____
5. We erased the third letter.   _____
6. We circled the fifth letter.   _____
7. We marked out the twenty-fifth letter. _____
8. We underlined the letter before l.   _____
9. We circled the first letter.   _____
10. We underlined the letter after e.   _____

2 A Listen

A._____  B._____  C._____  D._____

E._____  F._____  G._____

H._____  I._____  J._____  K._____

2 B Listen and write the letters.

1. ____
2. ____
3. ____
4. ____ ____
5. ____ ____

6. ____ ____
7. ____ ____ ____
8. ____ ____ ____
9. ____ ____ ____ ____
10. ____ ____ ____ ____

2 C Spelling. Write the words on the lines.

Simple past
Adjectives   **109**

GRAMMAR FOCUS

+d

Present	Past
erase	erase**d**
wave	wave**d**
underline	underline**d**

+ed

mark	mark**ed**
touch	touch**ed**
point	point**ed**

3 Write.

	Present	Past		Present	Past
1.	erase	*erased*	7.	wash	_____
2.	play	*played*	8.	listen	_____
3.	wave	_____	9.	shave	_____
4.	circle	_____	10.	shower	_____
5.	point	_____	11.	brush	_____
6.	paint	_____	12.	sew	_____

GRAMMAR FOCUS

I washed.   Did you wash?   I didn't wash.

4 Read and answer.

1. I brushed my teeth yesterday.   *True*
2. I kissed a monkey yesterday.   _____
3. I washed my hands yesterday.   _____
4. I played soccer yesterday.   _____
5. I listened to the radio yesterday.   _____
6. I played dominos yesterday.   _____
7. I watched television yesterday.   _____

8. I mailed a letter yesterday. _____
9. I played baseball yesterday. _____
10. I played tennis with a spider yesterday. _____
11. I cooked rice yesterday. _____
12. I received a letter yesterday. _____

> **GRAMMAR FOCUS**
>
> Did you cook yesterday?
> Yes, I cooked yesterday. = Yes, I did.
> No, I didn't cook yesterday. = No, I didn't.

5 A Read and answer

1. Did you eat and drink yesterday?   *Yes, I did.*
2. Did you eat a horse yesterday?   *No, I didn't.*
3. Did you sweep your home yesterday?   _____
4. Did you listen to the radio yesterday? _____
5. Did you shave your head yesterday?   _____
6. Did you sit on a chair yesterday?   _____
7. Did you write your name yesterday?   _____
8. Did you watch television yesterday? _____
9. Did you wear boxing gloves yesterday? _____
10. Did you touch your nose yesterday? _____
11. Did you go to a movie yesterday?   _____
12. Did you kiss your elbow yesterday? _____

5 B Listen and write.

Simple past
Adjectives

LESSON 2

simple past, affirmative and negative

1 A Listen.

A. _____

B. _____

C. _____

D. _____

E. _____

F. _____

G. _____

H. _____

I. _____

1 B Listen and write the letters.

1. ____
2. ____
3. ____
4. ____ ____

5. ____ ____
6. ____ ____ ____
7. ____ ____ ____
8. ____ ____ ____

1 C Spelling. Write the words on the blanks.

112   Chapter 9

2 Read and answer.

1. There weren't any cars 200 years ago. _True_
2. There weren't any horses 200 years ago. _____
3. There weren't any cameras 200 years ago. _____
4. There weren't any airplanes 200 years ago. _____
5. There weren't any light bulbs 200 years ago. _____
6. There weren't any needles 200 years ago. _____
7. There weren't any computers 200 years ago. _____
8. There weren't any telephones 200 years ago. _____
9. There weren't any microwave ovens 200 years ago. _____
10. There weren't any radios 200 years ago. _____
11. There weren't any candles 200 years ago. _____
12. There weren't any brooms 200 years ago. _____

3 Write sentences.

1. books / televisions
   People had books 200 years ago, but they didn't have televisions.
2. horses / cars
   _____
3. candles / light bulbs
   _____
4. letters / e-mails
   _____
5. glasses / contact lenses
   _____
6. newspapers / radios
   _____

Simple past
Adjectives

4 A   Listen.

A. _____

B. _____

C. _____

D. _____

E. _____

F. _____

G. _____

H. _____

I. _____

4 B   Listen and write the letters.

1. ____
2. ____
3. ____ ____
4. ____ ____
5. ____ ____
6. ____ ____ ____
7. ____ ____ ____
8. ____ ____ ____ ____

4 C   Spelling. Write the words on the blanks.

114   Chapter 9

5 Read and answer.

32°F 0°C	 32°F 0°C	 50°F 10°C	 50°F 10°C
Sunday	Monday	Tuesday	Wednesday TODAY

75°F 24°C	 75°F 24°C	 75°F 24°C
Thursday	Friday	Saturday

1. Today is a cool, rainy day.   *True*
2. Yesterday was a windy, cool day. _____
3. Tomorrow will be a cloudy, hot day. _____
4. Monday was a windy, cold day. _____
5. Sunday was a snowy, cold day. _____
6. Friday will be a sunny, warm day. _____
7. Tuesday was a cold, windy day. _____
8. Friday and Saturday will be warm, sunny days. _____

Simple past
Adjectives

LESSON 3
Adjectives

1 A Listen.

A.  _____ B.  _____ C.  _____ D.  _____ E. _____

75°F 38°C
50°F 10°C
32°F 0°C

F. _____ G.  _____ H.  _____ I.  _____ J. _____

1 B Listen and write the letters.

1. ____
2. ____
3. ____
4. ____ ____
5. ____ ____
6. ____ ____
7. ____ ____
8. ____ ____ ____
9. ____ ____ ____
10. ____ ____ ____ ____

1 C Spelling. Write the words on the blanks.

116   Chapter 9

2 A Listen.

A. _____ people

B. _____ people

C. _____ basketball players

D. _____ basketball players

E. _____ suitcase

F. _____ suitcase

G. _____ temperature

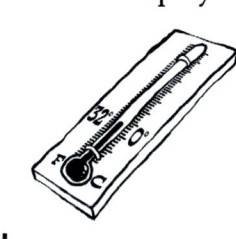

H. _____ temperature

I. _____ clothes

J. _____ clothes

K. _____ animals

L. _____ animals

M. _____ car

N. _____ car

O. _____ hair

P. _____ hair

2 B Listen and write the letters.

1. ____
2. ____
3. ____
4. ____ ____
5. ____ ____
6. ____ ____
7. ____ ____
8. ____ ____
9. ____ ____ ____
10. ____ ____ ____ ____

2 C Spelling. Write the words on the blanks.

Simple past
Adjectives   117

	GRAMMAR FOCUS	
	Adjective	Noun
a	big	animal
	new	clothes

3 Look at the words. Write in the blanks.

1. a ____*high*____ temperature
2. a _____ elephant
3. _____ clothes
4. a _____ turtle
5. a _____ summer
6. _____ hair
7. a _____ suitcase
8. a _____ mouse
9. a _____ basketball player
10. a _____ winter

big
cold
heavy
high
hot
little
long
old
slow
tall

GRAMMAR FOCUS	
	Adjective ↓
Elephants are	big.
January is	cold.

4 Read and write.

1. The grandfathers aren't young.   *They're old.*
2. The car isn't slow.   *It's fast.*
3. Elephants aren't little.   _____
4. Her hair isn't long.   _____
5. The suitcases aren't light.   _____
6. The clothes aren't new.   _____
7. The temperature isn't high.   _____
8. Summer isn't cold.   _____
9. The basketball players aren't short.   _____
10. A turtle isn't fast.   _____

GRAMMAR FOCUS

little = small   A mouse is **little**. = A mouse is **small**.
big = large   An elephant is **big**. = An elephant is **large**.

5 A Write.

1. a mouse — *A mouse is small.*
2. July and August — *July and August are hot.*
3. basketball players _____
4. winters _____
5. a turtle _____
6. March _____
7. a baby _____
8. elephants _____

5 B Listen and put in 21 carets (ʌ).

Anna: Grandmother, when you born?
Grandmother: I born in 1921.
Anna: You watch a lot of television when you a girl?
Grandmother: No, people didn't televisions. They listened the radio.
Anna: People have cars?
Grandmother: Oh, yes, there a lot of cars. My family had an old black car.
Anna: How about? Did you a computer?
Grandmother: No, there any computers. We didn't video games like you today.
Anna: What about movies? You go to the movies?
Grandmother: Oh, yes, there movies, but they in color.
Anna: No color! They have color?
Grandmother: No, they. It all black and white.
Anna: Movies color! Grandmother, is that?

5 C Write these words above the carets.

computers   did   did   did   didn't   didn't   do   have   have   play   to

true   was   was   were   were   were   were   weren't   weren't   without

Simple past
Adjectives

10 Comparatives

LESSON 1

larger, smaller

1 A Listen.

A.	100	B.	1,000	C.	10,000
D.	20,000	E.	100,000	F.	1,000,000
G.	10,000,000	H.	100,000,000	I.	1,000,000,000

1 B Listen and write the letters.

1. _____
2. _____
3. _____

4. _____ _____
5. _____ _____
6. _____ _____ _____

2 A Listen and circle.

1.	1,198	(1,189)	1,098
2.	30,474	30,447	34,447
3.	106,000	160,000	100,600
4.	582,000	508,200	500,820
5.	724,350	734,350	754,350
6.	1,299,000	1,289,000	1,298,000
7.	11,114,000	11,141,000	11,441,000
8.	300,836,000	308,836,000	300,863,000
9.	4,540,000,000	4,504,000,000	4,450,000,000
10.	62,490,742,000	62,480,742,000	62,498,742,000

120   Chapter 10

GRAMMAR FOCUS

1,000 = one thousand   1,000,000 = one million   1,000,000,000 = one billion

2 B Read and write.

1. ten thousand six hundred — *10,600*
2. four hundred fifty thousand eight hundred forty — _____
3. nine million, three hundred sixty thousand — _____
4. seventy million, five hundred thirty thousand — _____
5. seventeen million, one hundred ninety thousand nine hundred twenty — _____
6. three billion, five hundred fifty million, two hundred sixteen thousand — _____

2 C Listen and write.

1. *9,363,000*
2. _____
3. _____
4. _____
5. _____
6. _____
7. _____
8. _____
9. _____
10. _____

3 A Listen.

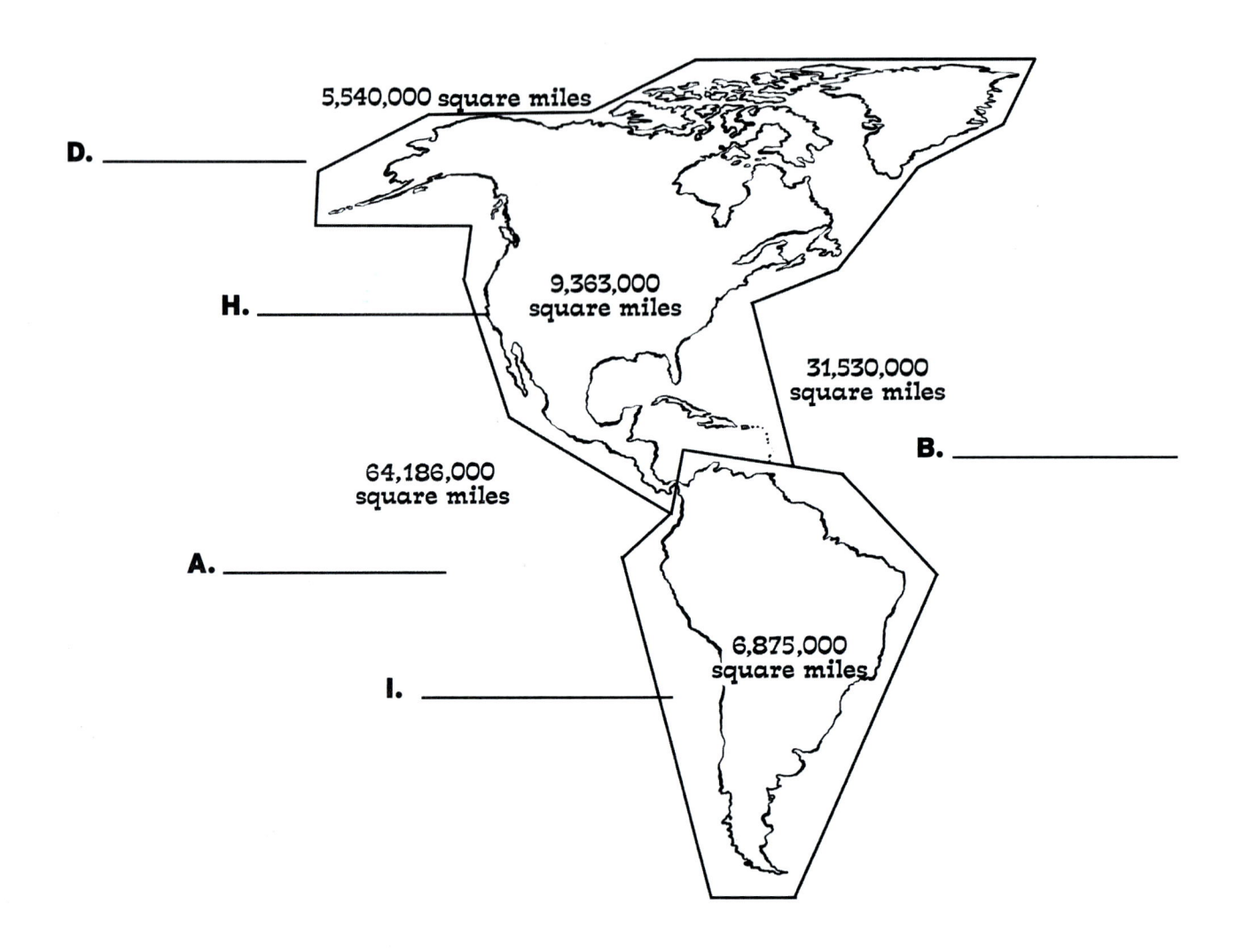

5,540,000 square miles

D. _____

9,363,000 square miles

H. _____

31,530,000 square miles

B. _____

64,186,000 square miles

A. _____

6,875,000 square miles

I. _____

3 B Listen and write the letters.

1. ____
2. ____
3. ____ ____
4. ____ ____
5. ____ ____

6. ____ ____ ____
7. ____ ____ ____
8. ____ ____ ____
9. ____ ____ ____
10. ____ ____ ____ ____

3 C Spelling. Write the words on the blanks.

122   Chapter 10

GRAMMAR FOCUS

The Atlantic Ocean is *large*.   The Pacific Ocean is *larger*.
The Pacific Ocean is *larger than* the Atlantic Ocean.

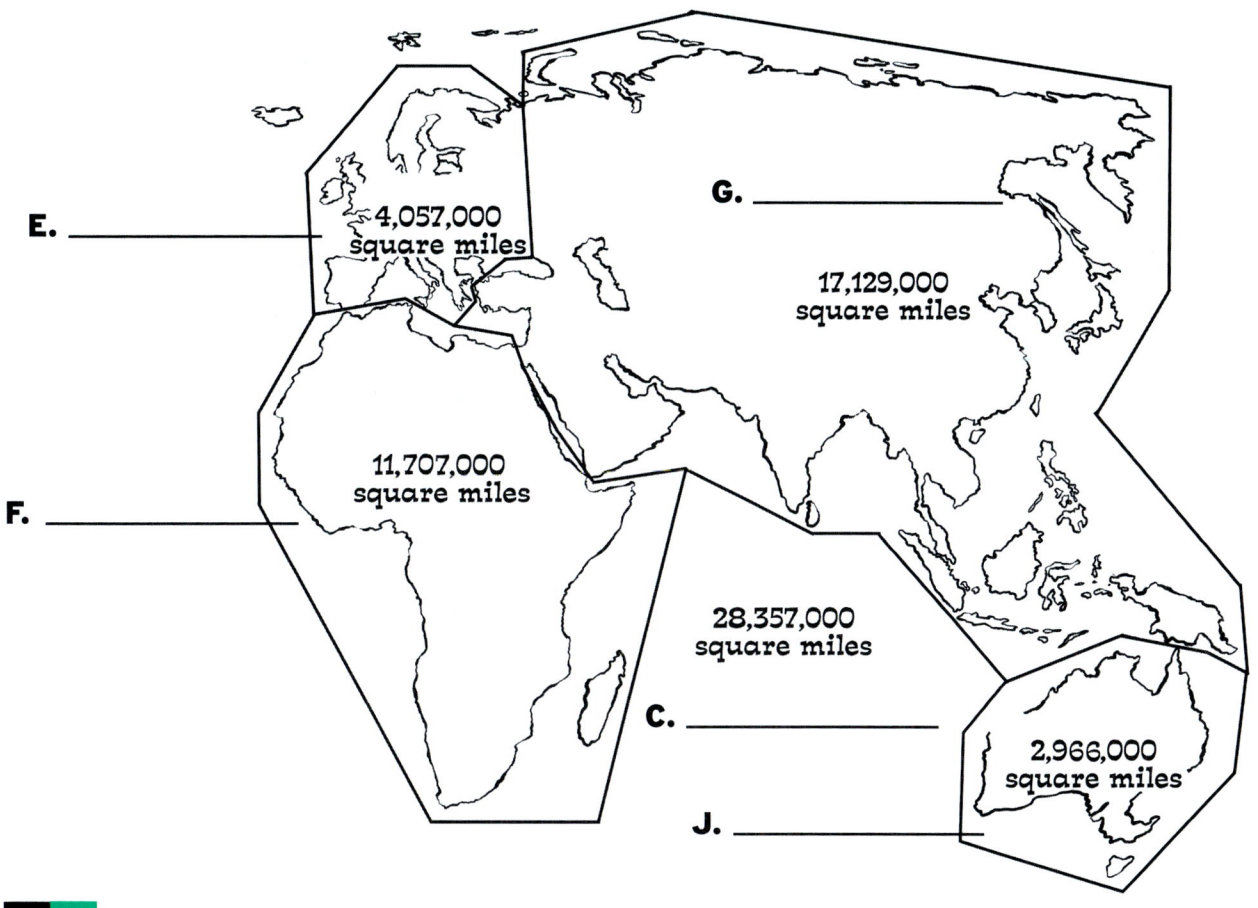

E. _____
4,057,000 square miles

G. _____
17,129,000 square miles

F. _____
11,707,000 square miles

C. _____
28,357,000 square miles

J. _____
2,966,000 square miles

3 D Read and answer.

1. Africa is larger than South America. ____True____
2. Asia is larger than North America. _____
3. The Pacific Ocean is smaller than the Atlantic Ocean. _____
4. The Indian Ocean is smaller than the Arctic Ocean. _____
5. Europe is larger than North America. _____
6. Africa is smaller than Australia. _____
7. The Arctic Ocean is smaller than the Pacific Ocean. _____
8. South America is larger than Europe. _____
9. The Atlantic Ocean is smaller than the Indian Ocean. _____
10. Asia is larger than Europe and Australia. _____

3 E With a partner, read and answer 3D.

LESSON 2

-er adjectives with *than*
the same as

1 A   Listen.

A. _____   B. _____   C. _____   D. _____

E. _____   F. _____   G. _____

H. _____   I. _____   J. _____   K. _____

1 B   Listen and write the letters.

1. ____
2. ____
3. ____ ____
4. ____ ____

5. ____
6. ____
7. ____ ____

8. ____ ____ ____
9. ____ ____ ____
10. ____ ____ ____

1 C   Spelling. Write the words on the blanks.

124   Chapter 10

2 A Read and answer.

1. Is a motorcycle faster than a bicycle?   _Yes_
2. Is a cow faster than a horse?   _____
3. Is a train slower than an airplane?   _____
4. Is an elephant slower than a deer?   _____
5. Is a bicycle slower than a car?   _____
6. Is a turtle faster than a rabbit?   _____
7. Is a truck slower than an airplane?   _____
8. Is a deer faster than a cow?   _____
9. Is a truck slower than a car?   _____
10. Is a motorcycle faster than a horse?   _____

2 B Listen and answer.

3 Write sentences.

1. deer / cow
   A deer is faster than a cow.

2. trucks / cars
   Trucks are slower than cars.

3. bicycle / motorcycle
   _____

4. turtle / rabbit
   _____

5. airplane / train
   _____

6. car / bicycle
   _____

7. cow / horse
   _____

8. car / truck
   _____

Comparatives   125

4 Read and answer.

1. The older boy is taller than the younger boy.   _True_
2. A small suitcase is heavier than a big suitcase.   _____
3. May is warmer than July.   _____
4. A mother is older than her daughter.   _____
5. February is shorter than January.   _____
6. Cars are larger than trucks.   _____
7. Snowy days are colder than rainy days.   _____
8. London is older than New York.   _____
9. 32°F is higher than 0°C.   _____
10. Summer is hotter than spring.   _____

5 A Class Activity. Make a chart. List your height and/or age.

	feet and inches	meters and centimeters	age
Juan	5'11"	1m 80cm	18
Maria	5'6"	1m 68cm	19

5 B With a partner, write sentences.

Juan is taller than Maria.
Maria is shorter than Juan.
Juan is younger than Maria.
Maria is older than Juan.

126   Chapter 10

6 A Listen.

A.   B.   C.   D.   E.

6 B Listen and write the letters.

1. ____
2. ____
3. ____ ____
4. ____ ____
5. ____ ____ ____
6. ____ ____ ____
7. ____ ____ ____ ____
8. ____ ____ ____ ____ ____

GRAMMAR FOCUS

1 penny = 1 cent.
A penny is **the same as** 1 cent.
1 nickel = 5 cents.
A nickel is **the same as** 5 cents.

6 C Read and answer.

1. A dime is the same as 10 cents.   *True*
2. A quarter is the same as 2 dimes.   _____
3. A nickel is the same as 5 cents.   _____
4. A penny is the same as 1 cent.   _____
5. Three dimes are the same as 1 quarter.   _____
6. Four quarters are the same as 1 dollar.   _____
7. Three nickels are the same as 2 dimes.   _____
8. Two dimes and a nickel are the same as 1 quarter.   _____
9. Ten dimes are the same as 8 quarters.   _____
10. One dollar is the same as 2 quarters,
    4 dimes, and 2 nickels.   _____

Comparatives   127

LESSON 3

more/less than
more/fewer than

GRAMMAR FOCUS

an ounce = 1 ounce
a pound = 1 pound

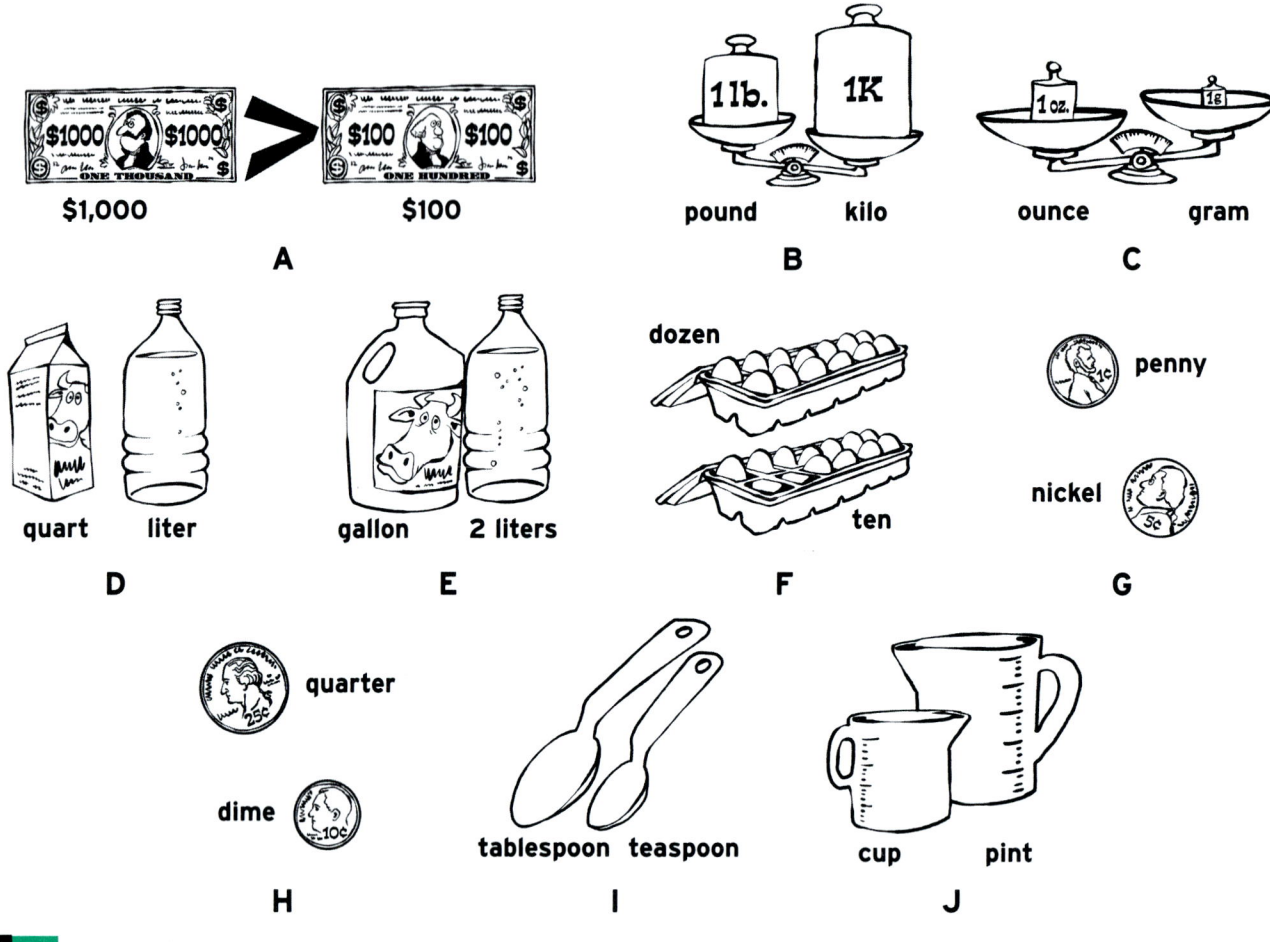

1 A Listen.

A. $1,000 > $100
B. pound   kilo
C. ounce   gram
D. quart   liter
E. gallon   2 liters
F. dozen   ten
G. penny   nickel
H. quarter   dime
I. tablespoon   teaspoon
J. cup   pint

1 B Read and answer.

1. Is a liter more or less than a quart? _more_
2. Is an ounce more or less than a gram? _____
3. Is a nickel more or less than a penny? _____
4. Is a tablespoon more or less than a teaspoon? _____
5. Is a kilo more or less than a pound? _____
6. Is a gallon more or less than two liters? _____
7. Is a dime more or less than a quarter? _____
8. Is a dozen more or less than ten? _____
9. Is a cup more or less than a pint? _____
10. Is a quarter more or less than two dimes? _____

128 Chapter 10

GRAMMAR FOCUS

The big car costs **more** than the small car.   The small car costs **less** than the big car.

2 A Read and answer.

1. Does a car cost more than a motorcycle? _____Yes_____
2. Does a gallon of milk cost less than a liter of milk? _____
3. Does a pound of potatoes cost more than a kilo of potatoes? _____
4. Does a dozen eggs cost less than ten eggs? _____
5. Does a pencil cost more than a book? _____
6. Does a television cost more than a radio? _____
7. Does a shirt cost less than a jacket? _____
8. Does a belt cost more than shoes? _____
9. Does a piano cost more than a guitar? _____
10. Does a tennis ball cost more than a soccer ball? _____

2 B Write.

1. televisions / radios _____Televisions cost more than radios._____
2. old cars / new cars _____Old cars cost less than new cars._____
3. computers / books _____
4. two liters of milk / two quarts of milk _____
5. pencils / pens _____
6. two pounds of apples / two kilos of apples _____
7. twenty sheets of paper / a dozen sheets of paper _____
8. horses / dogs _____
9. big trucks / small trucks _____
10. gloves / a jacket _____

Comparatives **129**

3 A Listen.

Map populations:
- Toronto 2,385,000
- Montreal 1,036,000
- Chicago 2,896,000
- New York 8,008,000
- Los Angeles 3,694,000
- Mexico City 8,591,000
- Bogota 6,712,000
- Rio de Janeiro 5,850,000
- Cairo 6,789,000
- Beijing 7,362,000
- Seoul 10,310,000
- Tokyo 8,130,000

GRAMMAR FOCUS

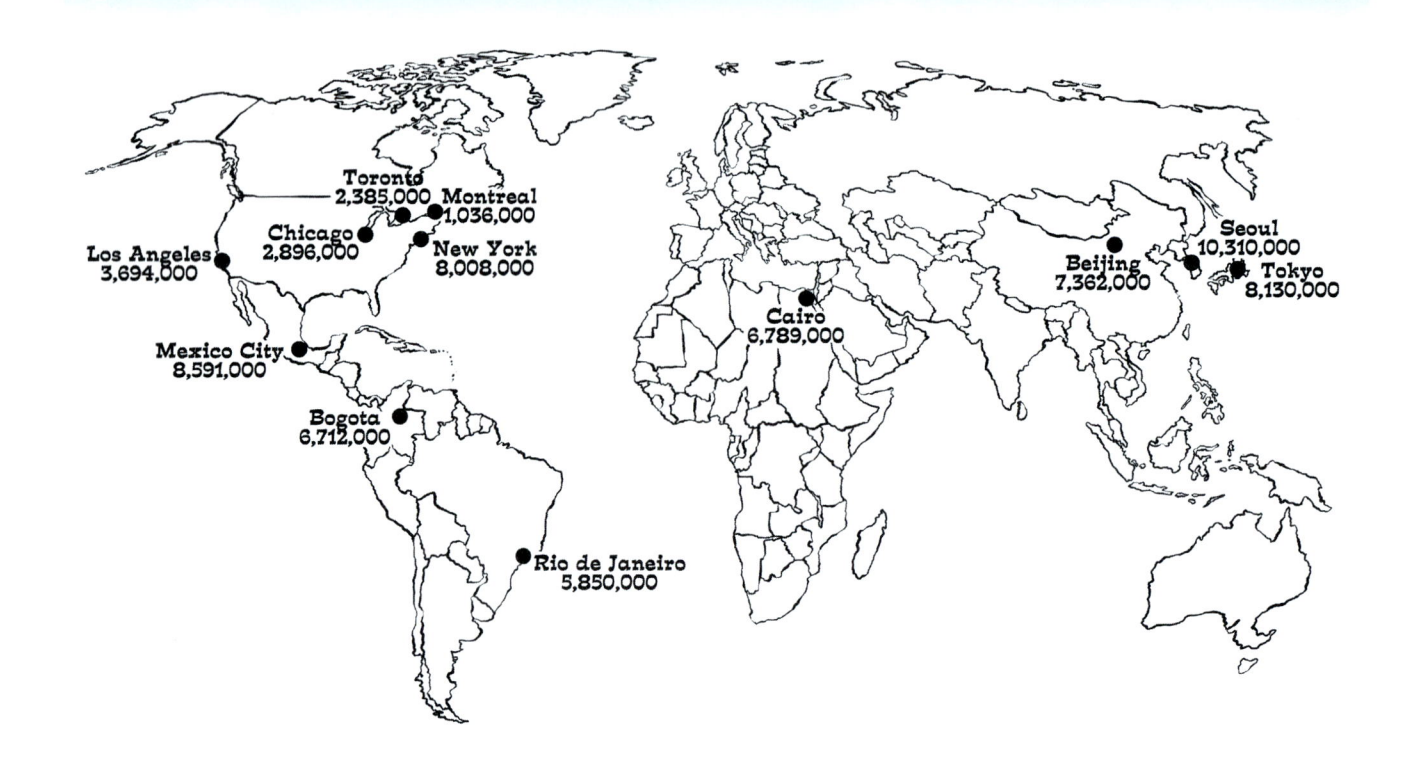

New York has **more** people than Chicago.
Chicago has **fewer** people than New York.
There are **more** people in New York **than** in Chicago.
There are **fewer** people in Chicago **than** in New York.

3 B Read and write.

1. Does New York have more people than Mexico City? _No_
2. Are there fewer people in Chicago than in Bogota? _Yes_
3. Does Los Angeles have fewer people than Montreal? _____
4. Are there more people in Seoul than in Rio de Janeiro? _____
5. Are there fewer people in Beijing than in Tokyo? _____
6. Does Toronto have more people than Chicago? _____
7. Does Cairo have fewer people than Los Angeles? _____
8. Are there fewer people in Bogota than in Seoul? _____
9. Are there more people in Tokyo than in New York? _____
10. Does Mexico City have fewer people than Toronto? _____

Chapter 10

4 A Make a chart.

	sisters	brothers
Juan	1	2
Maria		3
Paul	2	1

4 B With a partner, write sentences.

Juan has fewer brothers than Maria.

Maria has more brothers than Juan.

Juan and Maria have more brothers than Paul.

5 A Listen and put in 25 carets (∧).

When I was 16, sister was 14. She was one year 11 months than I was. We basketball and soccer. My sister was than the other players. She long arms and long legs. I was than the other players, and I had arms and short legs. My sister was a very basketball player but I. From March to May played soccer. My legs were, but I was. I was faster the tall girls. I was a soccer player, but my sister.

Today I two daughters. One plays basketball, one plays soccer. My sister and I watch my when they play, and we are. We of the days when we were and played basketball and soccer. One of my daughters is, and one is. But the one is good at soccer, and the one is good at basketball.

5 B Write these words above the carets.

and	daughters	fast	good	good	had	happy	have	my
played	short	short	short	shorter	shorter	tall	taller
taller	than	think	wasn't	wasn't	we	young	younger

Comparatives   131

11 Objects, Object pronouns

LESSON 1
object pronouns

1

2

1 Read and answer.

1. Can we see Bill in photo 1? _Yes_
2. Can we see him in photo 2? _No_
3. Can we see him in photo 3? _____
4. Can we see him in photo 4? _____
5. Can we see Bill's sister in photo 1? _____
6. Can we see her in photo 2? _____
7. Can we see her in photo 3? _____
8. Can we see her in photo 4? _____

3

4

9. Can we see Bill's parents in photo 1? _____

10. Can we see them in photo 2? _____

11. Can we see them in photo 3? _____

12. Can we see them in photo 4? _____

13. Can we see the horse's head in photo 1? _____

14. Can we see it in photo 2? _____

15. Can we see it in photo 3? _____

16. Can we see it in photo 4? _____

2 A Listen.

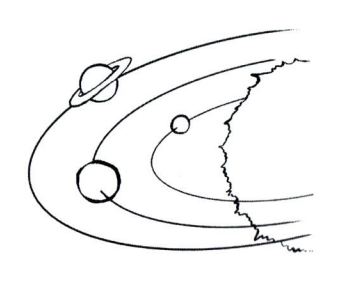

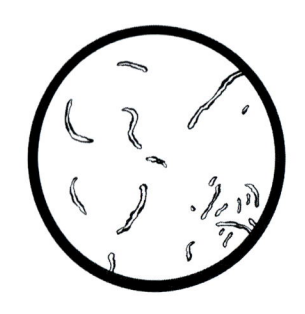

A. _____ B. _____ C. _____

D. _____ E. _____ F. _____ G. _____

H. _____ I. _____ J. _____

2 B Listen and write the letters.

1. ____
2. ____
3. ____ ____
4. ____ ____

5. ____ ____ ____
6. ____ ____ ____
7. ____ ____ ____ ____
8. ____ ____ ____ ____

2 C Spelling. Write the words on the blanks.

134   Chapter 11

GRAMMAR FOCUS

Can you see Bill's mother?
Yes, I can see **her**.

Can you see Bill?
Yes, I can see **him**.

Can you see Bill's mother and father?
Yes, I can see **them**.

Can you see Bill's horse?
Yes, I can see **it**.

3 Read and answer.

1. Can we see the planets with a telescope? _Yes_
2. Can we see the sun at night? _____
3. Can we see microbes without a microscope? _____
4. Can we see the moon at night? _____
5. Can we see the stars in the day? _____
6. Can we see the moon without a telescope? _____
7. Can we see mountains with a telescope? _____
8. Can we see the planets with a microscope? _____

4 Write answers.

1. Can we see the stars in the day?
   No, but we can see them at night.

2. Can we see snow in summer?
   No, but we can see it in winter.

3. Can we see the planets with a microscope?
   _____

4. Can we see the sun at night?
   _____

5. Can we see microbes with a telescope?
   _____

6. Can we see mountains with a microscope?
   _____

Objects, object pronouns **135**

LESSON 2
objects

1 A Listen.

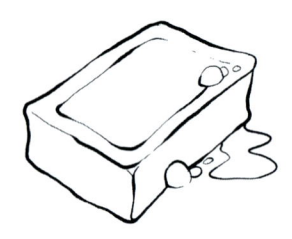

A. _____   B. _____   C. _____

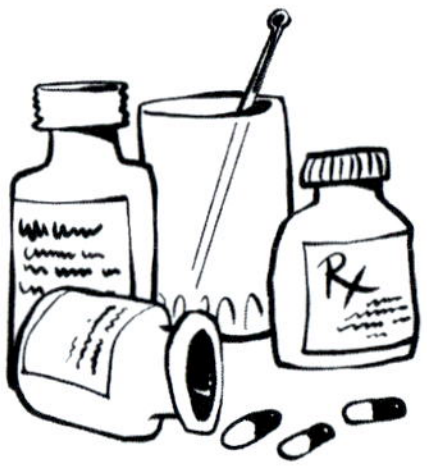

D. _____   E. _____   F. _____   G. _____

H. _____   I. _____   J. _____

1 B Listen and write the letters.

1. ____
2. ____
3. ____ ____
4. ____ ____
5. ____ ____

6. ____ ____ ____
7. ____ ____ ____
8. ____ ____ ____
9. ____ ____ ____ ____

1 C Spelling. Write the words on the blanks.

136   Chapter 11

2 A Write the word.

1. My aunt is thirsty. Does she need water or medicine? _water_
2. We are dirty. Do we need food or soap? _____
3. My hands are cold. Do I need a jacket or gloves? _____
4. The boy is lost. Does he need a map or a jacket? _____
5. Her cousins are hungry. Do they need water or food? _____
6. The girl is tired. Does she need food or sleep? _____
7. The plant is dry. Does it need milk or water? _____
8. The boy is wet. Does he need a shirt or a towel? _____
9. My niece is sick. Does she need medicine or soap? _____
10. The children are dirty. Do they need food and medicine or soap and water? _____

2 B Read and write.

food   a jacket   a map   medicine   sleep   soap   a towel   water

1. What do you need when you are dirty? _soap_
2. What do you drink when you are thirsty? _____
3. What do you need when you are sick? _____
4. What do you eat when you are hungry? _____
5. What do you need when you are lost? _____
6. What do you wear when you are cold? _____
7. What do you need when you are wet? _____
8. What do you need when you are tired? _____

> **GRAMMAR FOCUS**
>
> | | |
> |---|---|
> | I am lost. | Please give **me** a map. |
> | He is lost. | Please give **him** a map. |
> | She is lost. | Please give **her** a map. |
> | We are lost. | Please give **us** a map. |
> | They are lost. | Please give **them** a map. |

3 Write.

1. My aunt is thirsty.
   Please give her some water.

2. My son is wet.

3. We are dirty.

4. His cousins are hungry.

5. Her grandfather is sick.

6. I am thirsty.

7. Our niece and nephew are wet.

8. Rita and I are hungry.

9. My grandmother is sick.

10. Their hands are cold.

4 A Class Activity. Give your book and 2 pencils to the person behind you. Answer questions.

Teacher: Maria, who has your book?
Maria: Juan has *it*.
Teacher: Maria, who has your pencils?
Maria: Juan has *them*.

4 B Half of the class stand up. Turn and face the back of the room. Answer questions.

Teacher: Maria, can you see Juan?
Maria: Yes, I can see *him*.
Teacher: Keiko, can you see Maria and Paul?
Maria: No, I can't see *them*.

4 C With a partner, write sentences.

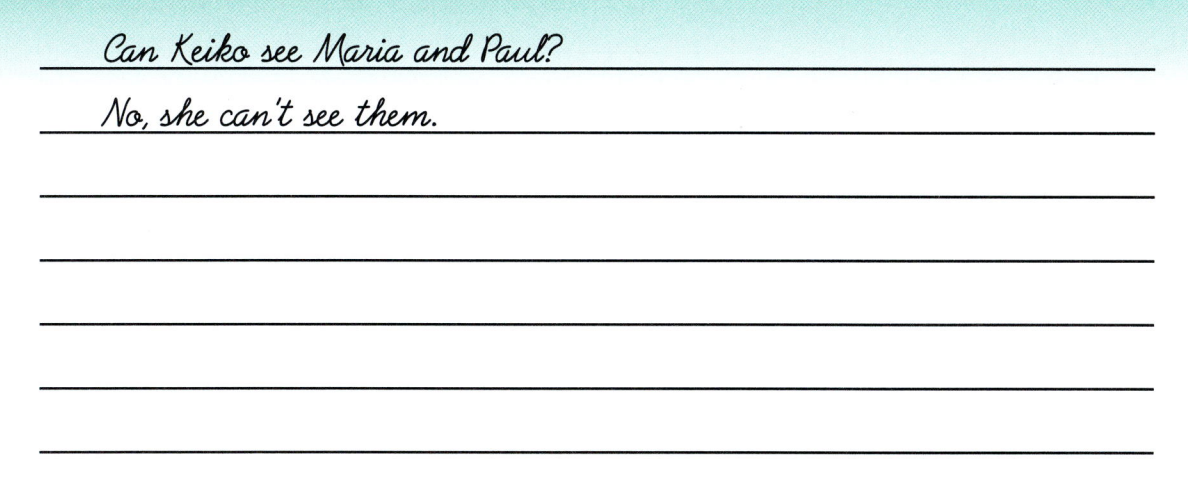

Can Keiko see Maria and Paul?
No, she can't see them.

LESSON 3
object pronouns
get

1 A Listen.

A. _____

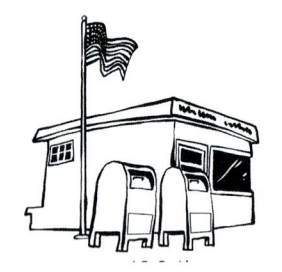

B. _____

C. _____

D. _____

E. _____

F. _____

G. _____

H. _____

I. _____

1 B Listen and write the letters.

1. _____
2. _____
3. _____ _____
4. _____ _____

5. _____ _____
6. _____ _____ _____
7. _____ _____ _____
8. _____ _____ _____ _____

1 C Spelling. Write the words on the blanks.

140   Chapter 11

2 Read and answer.

1. Do we get clothes at the mall? ___Yes___
2. Do we get stamps at the post office? _____
3. Do we get pizza at the jewelry store? _____
4. Do we get shoes at the library? _____
5. Do we get bread at the bakery? _____
6. Do we get cars at the hardware store? _____
7. Do we get watches at the jewelry store? _____
8. Do we get books at the library? _____
9. Do we get tools at the hardware store? _____
10. Do we get medicine at the drugstore? _____

3 A Read and write.

1. Please go with her to the supermarket. ___She will get you some food.___
2. Please go with them to the bakery. _____
3. Please go with us to the post office. _____
4. Please go with my father to the hardware store. _____
5. Please go with him and me to the jewelry store. _____
6. Please go with her and him to the drugstore. _____

3 B Write.

1. They will get her some bread if _she_ goes with _them_ to the bakery.
2. We will get him some food if _____ goes with _____ to the supermarket.
3. She will get them some tools if _____ go with _____ to the hardware store.
4. He will get us some medicine if _____ go with _____ to the drugstore.
5. I will get you some stamps if _____ go with _____ to the post office.
6. You will get her a watch if _____ goes with _____ to the jewelry store.
7. We will get you some books if _____ go with _____ to the library.
8. Her grandparents will get her some clothes if _____ goes with _____ to the mall.

4 A Listen and put in 19 carets (∧).

Linda: John, stop television and listen. I'm going to drive to school in minutes.

John: Yes, Mother.

Linda: Do you your jacket?

John: Yes, I have.

Linda: Do you have books?

John: Yes, I have.

Linda: John, stop watching television listen.

John: Listening.

Linda: Did you your teeth?

John: Yes, I brushed.

Linda: Did wash your face?

John: Yes, I washed.

Linda: Can you see your in the car?

John: Yes, I can see.

Linda: Can you see your in the car?

John: Yes, I can see.

Linda: Well, then. Get your and let's.

4 B Write these words above the carets.

| and | books | brush | father | five | go | have | her | him | I'm |
| it | it | sister | them | them | watching | you | you | your | |

142   Chapter 11

5 A Find these words. Circle.

BREAD	FOOD	MEDICINE	WATCHES	TOOLS
BOOKS	CLOTHES	STAMPS	JEWELRY	HARDWARE
BAKERY	SUPERMARKET	DRUGSTORE	LIBRARY	MALL

```
T B R D O S Y E E C T E W D J
E F O W Z R X R Y E T E A E E
D G G O A W O Y E E M H T M W
M M P R K T C S K P W C C E E
L V B A S S P R F N G T H D L
M I E G Y M A Q Y Z G A E I R
L N U Q A M C N F K S W S C Y
V R C T R B L B R E A D K I T
D Y S E S A O S T O O T V N Y
M G P K P K T T O A M Q M E U
K U H L M E H E O I C I D A O
S U L A W R E G L H F O O D G
A A N O T Y S L S J O Z Q I F
M K T O S P N P C E R M F V P
H A R D W A R E G M S O E R M
```

5 B With a partner, write these words in alphabetical order.

bakery _____ _medicine_

_____ _hardware_ _____

_____ _____ _____

_____ _____ _____

_____ _____ _____

Objects, object pronouns   143

12 Summary

1 A Listen.

| car   boy   book
arm   pencil |
|---|

A _____

| gloves   numbers   ears
hands   children |
|---|

B _____

| are   has   writes
eat   is   does |
|---|

C _____

| shaved   had   played
was   did |
|---|

D _____

| in   above   on
under   of   with |
|---|

E _____

| hot   dirty   old
large   hungry |
|---|

F _____

| I   you   it
she   him   me |
|---|

G _____

| we   them   you
they   us |
|---|

H _____

1 B Listen and write the letters.

1. ____
2. ____
3. ____
4. ____ ____

5. ____ ____
6. ____ ____
7. ____ ____ ____
8. ____ ____ ____

1 C Spelling. Write the words on the blanks.

144   Chapter 12

2 A Read and answer.

1. Is *old* an adjective? _____Yes_____
2. Are *eat* and *sleep* present tense verbs? _____
3. Is *us* a plural pronoun? _____
4. Are *pencils* and *books* singular nouns? _____
5. Is *was* a present tense verb? _____
6. Are *boy* and *girl* plural nouns? _____
7. Are *hot* and *clean* adjectives? _____
8. Are *on* and *in* prepositions? _____
9. Are *is* and *am* past tense verbs? _____
10. Is *he* a singular pronoun? _____

2 B Read and circle.

#	Sentence	Option 1	Option 2
1.	The <u>girls</u> are from Toronto.	singular noun	**(plural noun)**
2.	The cars <u>are</u> old.	present-tense verb	past-tense verb
3.	<u>We</u> eat potatoes.	singular pronoun	plural pronoun
4.	He <u>was</u> happy yesterday.	present-tense verb	past-tense verb
5.	The <u>children</u> will play soccer.	singular noun	plural noun
6.	Lydia is going with <u>her</u>.	singular pronoun	plural pronoun
7.	We are wearing <u>dirty</u> clothes.	adjective	noun
8.	They go to school <u>with</u> Anna.	adjective	preposition
9.	She is drinking <u>cold</u> water.	adjective	noun
10.	<u>He</u> has my books.	noun	pronoun

Summary

3 **Write these words on the correct lines.**

above	car	does	gloves	hot	me	them	washed
after	children	ears	had	hungry	on	they	we
am	cold	eats	hands	I	pen	thirsty	were
are	cooked	eyes	have	in	she	truck	with
arm	did	from	~~he~~	it	shoes	us	
boy	do	girl	her	large	small	was	

_he_ _____
_____
_____
_____

SINGULAR — **PLURAL**

Pronouns — **WORD** — **Nouns**

SINGULAR — **PLURAL**

GROUPS

- **Adjectives**
  - _____
  - _____
  - _____
  - _____
  - _____
  - _____
  - _____

- **Prepositions**
  - _____
  - _____
  - _____
  - _____

- **Verbs**

PRESENT TENSE
- _____
- _____
- _____
- _____
- _____

PAST TENSE
- _____
- _____
- _____
- _____
- _____

Back of the Book

The Basics

LESSON 1

PAGE 2 1. A. Say the following numbers three times, pausing briefly after each number.

| zero | two | four | six | eight | ten |
| one | three | five | seven | nine | |

PAGE 2 1. B. Read the following numbers. The students circle the numbers read.

1. two
2. six
3. zero seven
4. two eight
5. four seven
6. three five eight
7. zero five seven
8. six eight nine
9. three two one four
10. four six seven zero

PAGE 2 2. Read the following math sentences. The students write the missing numbers on the lines provided.

1. Two plus two equals four.
2. Four plus five equals nine.
3. Seven plus three equals ten.
4. Eight minus six equals two.
5. Nine minus three equals six.
6. Ten minus eight equals two.
7. Three times two equals six.
8. Two times five equals ten.
9. Ten divided by two equals five.
10. Nine divided by three equals three.

PAGE 3 3. Read the following telephone numbers. The students write the missing numbers on the lines provided. (0 is often pronounced "oh" [o] in telephone numbers.)

A.
1. 828-5791 (eight two eight five seven nine one)
2. 527-5172
3. 452-9555
4. 378-4391
5. 820-7331
6. 747-4396
7. 473-3001
8. 242-0409
9. 921-0335
10. 365-5061

B.
1. 482-1913
2. 590-6473
3. 225-0057
4. 481-1299
5. 466-0900
6. 267-4632
7. 561-1540
8. 768-9334
9. 531-8222
10. 489-8070

PAGE 3 4. Read the following telephone numbers with area codes. The students write the missing numbers on the lines provided.

A.
1. 205-939-9934 (two oh five nine three nine nine nine three four)
2. 334-609-3540
3. 907-339-6231
4. 870-486-6592
5. 707-942-0954
6. 859-862-8684
7. 651-219-5953
8. 406-297-2655
9. 862-352-4918
10. 575-992-3568

B.
1. 303-562-5881
2. 785-233-0217
3. 801-946-8485
4. 989-579-2255
5. 701-438-3238
6. 307-448-3496
7. 976-325-6640
8. 780-246-2327
9. 506-764-3623
10. 250-387-0238

LESSON 2

PAGE 4 1. A. Say the alphabet three times, pausing briefly after each letter.

PAGE 4 **1. B.** Read the following letters. The students circle the letters read.

1. D
2. V
3. A B
4. M N
5. C H
6. T C H
7. A N T
8. C H E E
9. O U N D
10. A N K S

PAGE 4 **1. C.** Read the following letters. The students circle the letters read in each alphabet sequence.

1. B T
2. D O
3. F M T
4. E N W
5. A H O Y
6. E L P U
7. I Q V Z
8. A E I O U
9. G J R V X
10. C G I Q Y

Page 5 **2. A.** Spell each word. The students write the missing letters on the lines provided. For each one say the number, spell it, and then repeat it–for example, two, T W O, two.

1. two T W O two
2. ten T E N ten
3. six S I X six
4. one O N E one
5. zero Z E R O zero
6. nine N I N E nine
7. four F O U R four
8. five F I V E five
9. three T H R E E three
10. seven S E V E N seven
11. eight E I G H T eight

Chapter 1

LESSON 1

PAGE 6 1. A. Say the days of the week three times, pausing briefly after each day.

Sunday   Monday   Tuesday   Wednesday   Thursday   Friday   Saturday

PAGE 6 2. A. Spell the days of the week. The students write them on a sheet of paper.

1. Sunday S U N D A Y Sunday
2. Monday M O N D A Y Monday
3. Tuesday T U E S D A Y Tuesday
4. Wednesday W E D N E S D A Y Wednesday
5. Thursday T H U R S D A Y Thursday
6. Friday F R I D A Y Friday
7. Saturday S A T U R D A Y Saturday

PAGE 6 2. B. Read the following questions. The students write YES or NO on a sheet of paper.

1. Are there seven letters in *Sunday*?
2. Are there eight letters in *Thursday*?
3. Are there two *a*'s in *Saturday*?
4. Are there two *d*'s in *Wednesday*?
5. Is there one *a* in *Monday*?
6. Is there one *s* in *Tuesday*?
7. Is there one *e* in *Wednesday*?
8. Are there two *i*'s in *Friday*?
9. Are there two *u*'s in *Tuesday*?
10. Is there one *o* in *Monday*?
11. Is there one *r* in *Thursday*?
12. Are there two *s*'s in *Sunday*?

LESSON 2

PAGE 8 1. A. Read the following countries three times. Be sure to say the letter each time–for example: A. (pause) Canada, B. (pause) the United States, etc.

A. Canada
B. the United States
C. Mexico
D. Colombia
E. Brazil
F. England
G. France
H. Spain
I. Egypt
J. China
K. Korea
L. Japan

PAGE 8 1. B. Read the following. The students write the corresponding letters on the lines provided.

1. the United States
2. Spain
3. Japan
4. Mexico
5. China and France
6. Brazil and Colombia
7. Canada and Egypt
8. Korea and England
9. France, England, and Spain
10. Canada, Mexico, and the United States
11. Japan, Korea, and China
12. Colombia, Brazil, and Mexico

Instructions, Tapescripts   **149**

PAGE 10 2. A. Read the following cities three times. Be sure to say the number each time—for example: 1 (pause) Los Angeles, an American city, 2 (pause) Mexico City, a Mexican city, etc.

1. Los Angeles, an American city
2. Mexico City, a Mexican city
3. Bogota, a Colombian city
4. Montreal, a Canadian city
5. Toronto, a Canadian city
6. New York, an American city
7. Rio de Janeiro, a Brazilian city
8. London, an English city
9. Paris, a French city
10. Madrid, a Spanish city
11. Barcelona, a Spanish city
12. Cairo, an Egyptian city
13. Beijing, a Chinese city
14. Seoul, a Korean city
15. Tokyo, a Japanese city
16. Hong Kong, a Chinese city

PAGE 11 3. B. Read the questions of 3. A. The students write YES or NO on a sheet of paper.

LESSON 3

PAGE 12 1. A. Say I, we, you, you, he, she, they. Using the pictures as examples, tell students to stand in groups and practice pronouns.

PAGE 14 2. A. Read the following three times. Be sure to say the number each time—for example: 1. (pause) Mark, Canadian, 2. (pause) Angela, Canadian, etc.

1. Mark, Canadian
2. Angela, Canadian
3. Sam, American
4. Sara, American
5. Miguel, Mexican
6. Rosa, Mexican
7. Fernando, Colombian
8. Paulo, Brazilian
9. Sophie, French
10. Tarek, Egyptian
11. Ming, Chinese
12. Li, Chinese
13. Yung Sun, Korean
14. Keiko, Japanese

PAGE 15 2. C. Read the questions of 2. B. The students write YES or NO on a sheet of paper.

PAGE 17 1. B. Class Activity

Write the names of countries on cards and give each student one of the cards. Tell the students to pretend to be from the country on their cards. Then ask them questions. For example: Teacher: Maria, are you Korean? Maria: No, I'm not. I'm Canadian. Teacher: Paul, is Maria Korean? Paul: No, she isn't. She's Canadian.

PAGE 18 2. A. Read the following three times. Be sure to say the letter each time—for example: A (pause) cities, B (pause) countries, etc.

A. cities   B. countries   C. vowels   D. consonants   E. even numbers   F. odd numbers.

PAGE 18 2. B. Read the following. The students write the corresponding letters on the lines provided.

1. countries
2. odd numbers
3. consonants and vowels
4. countries and cities
5. even numbers, odd numbers, and vowels
6. cities, countries, and consonants

PAGE 18 2. C. Spell each word. The students write the words on the lines provided.

A. cities C I T I E S cities
B. countries C O U N T R I E S countries
C. vowels V O W E L S vowels
D. consonants C O N S O N A N T S consonants
E. even numbers even E V E N numbers N U M B E R S even numbers
F. odd numbers odd O D D numbers N U M B E R S odd numbers

PAGE 19 3. B. Read the questions of 3. A. The students write YES or NO on a sheet of paper.

Chapter 2

LESSON 1

PAGE 20 1. A. Read the following three times. Be sure to say the letter each time—for example: A (pause) pencil, B (pause) pen, etc.

A. pencil
B. pen
C. paper clip
D. map
E. book
F. sheet of paper
G. half sheet of paper.

150   Back of the Book

PAGE 20 1. B. Read the following. The students write the corresponding letters on the lines provided.

1. book
2. pen
3. map
4. sheet of paper
5. pen and pencil
6. half sheet of paper and map
7. book, pencil, and sheet of paper
8. pen, paper clip, and book

PAGE 20 1. C. Spell each word. The students write the words on the lines provided.

A. pencil P E N C I L pencil
B. pen P E N pen
C. paper clip paper P A P E R clip C L I P paper clip
D. map M A P map
E. book B O O K book
F. sheet of paper sheet S H E E T of O F paper P A P E R sheet of paper
G. half sheet of paper half H A L F sheet S H E E T of O F paper P A P E R half sheet of paper

PAGE 21 2. A. Read the following sentences three times, slightly stressing the prepositions in each sentence.

A. The pencil is on the book.
B. The pencil is in the book.
C. The pencil is under the book.
D. The pencil is to the right of the book.
E. The pencil is to the left of the book.
F. The pencil is between the books.
G. The pencil is above the book.

PAGE 21 2. B. Read the following. The students write the corresponding letters on the lines provided.

1. The pencil is in the book.
2. The pencil is under the book.
3. The pencil is between the books.
4. The pencil is on the book.
5. The pencil is to the right of the book.
6. The pencil is above the book.
7. The pencil is to the left of the book.

PAGE 21 2. C. Spell each word. The students write the words on the lines provided.

A. on O N on
B. in I N in
C. under U N D E R under
D. to the right of to T O the T H E right R I G H T of O F to the right of
E. to the left of to T O the T H E left L E F T of O F to the left of
F. between B E T W E E N between
G. above A B O V E above

PAGE 22 3. B. Read the commands of 3. B. Model for the students as needed.

PAGE 23 4. A. Read the following passage. Some words are in italics; these words are missing in the student section. Tell the students that there are nine words missing but that there are no spaces where those words are missing. Instruct the students to put a caret (∧) wherever there is a word missing. (The first caret has been placed for the students.)

Read the passage at least three times.

The pen is *under* the book The half sheet of paper is *on* the book. The map is *above* the book. The pencil is *in* the book. The sheet of paper is *to* the left *of* the book The paper clip is *to* the right *of* the book. The book is *between* the sheet of paper and the paper clip.

PAGE 23 4. B. After the students have put in all the carets in 4. A., instruct them to write the missing words above each caret.

LESSON 2

PAGE 24 1. A. Read the following parts of the body three times. Be sure to say the letter each time—for example: A. (pause) nose, B. (pause) eyes, etc.

A. nose
B. eyes
C. cheeks
D. mouth
E. ears
F. hair
G. teeth
H. head
I. chin
J. neck

Instructions, Tapescripts **151**

PAGE 24 1. B. Read the following. The students write the corresponding letters on the lines provided.

1. cheeks
2. hair
3. nose
4. eyes
5. mouth
6. teeth
7. head and neck
8. cheeks and mouth
9. eyes and teeth
10. nose and ears
11. hair, eyes, and cheeks
12. mouth, neck, and teeth

PAGE 24 1. C. Spell each word. The students write the words on the lines provided.

A. nose N O S E nose
B. eyes E Y E S eyes
C. cheeks C H E E K S cheeks
D. mouth M O U T H mouth
E. ears E A R S ears
F. hair H A I R hair
G. teeth T E E T H teeth
H. head H E A D head
I. chin C H I N chin
J. neck N E C K neck

PAGE 25 2. B. Read the questions of 2. A. The students write YES or NO on a sheet of paper.

PAGE 26 3. A. Pointing to the students in the seating chart of 3. A., say the following.

Sophie is in front of Rosa.
Sophie is behind Keiko.
Sophie is next to Paulo.
Sophie is next to Miguel.
Paulo is in front of Tarek.
Paulo is behind Li.
Paulo is next to Sophie.
Miguel is in front of Yung Sun.
Miguel is behind Fernando.
Miguel is next to Sophie.

LESSON 3

PAGE 28 1. A. Say the alphabet two times, asking the students to repeat each letter the second time.

PAGE 28 1. C. Dictate the alphabet. The students write the letters on a sheet of paper. Then read the questions of 1. B. The students write the answers on a sheet of paper.

PAGE 29 2. A. Say the following numbers two times.

10	13	16	19
11	14	17	20
12	15	18	

PAGE 29 2. C. Read the following years. The students circle the year they hear.

1. 1916 (read as nineteen sixteen)
2. 1813
3. 1721
4. 1909
5. 1214
6. 1222
7. 1121
8. 1015
9. 1312
10. 1602

PAGE 30 3. A. Say the following numbers two times.

| 10 | 30 | 50 | 70 | 90 |
| 20 | 40 | 60 | 80 | 100 (one hundred) |

PAGE 30 3. B. Read the following prices. The students circle the price they hear.

1. 26.95 (read as twenty-six, ninety-five)
2. 33.44
3. 48.41
4. 76.16
5. 88.12
6. 91.01
7. 59.13
8. 62.96
9. 12.04
10. 11.02

PAGE 31 4. A. Spell each word. The students write the words on the lines provided.

1. eleven E L E V E N eleven
2. twelve T W E L V E twelve
3. thirteen T H I R T E E N thirteen
4. twenty T W E N T Y twenty
5. thirty T H I R T Y thirty
6. forty F O R T Y forty
7. fifty F I F T Y fifty
8. sixty S I X T Y sixty
9. seventy S E V E N T Y seventy
10. eighty E I G H T Y eighty
11. ninety N I N E T Y ninety
12. one hundred O N E   H U N D R E D one hundred

PAGE 31 4. C. Read the questions of 4. B. The students write YES or NO on a sheet of paper.

152 Back of the Book

LESSON 4

PAGE 32 1. A. Read the following commands. The students draw lines between the numbers and the letters.

Draw a line from 3 to D.	Draw a line from 24 to Z.
Draw a line from 9 to H.	Draw a line from 8 to E.
Draw a line from 13 to P.	Draw a line from 10 to J.
Draw a line from 15 to Q.	Draw a line from 12 to M.
Draw a line from 22 to T.	Draw a line from 23 to X.

PAGE 33 2. A. Read the descriptions of each picture three times. Be sure to say the letter each time—for example, A. (pause) without a nose, B. (pause) without eyes, etc.

A. without a nose C. with a hat E. with teeth
B. without eyes D. without hair F. with glasses

PAGE 33 2. B. Read the following. The students write the corresponding letters on the lines provided.

1. without a nose
2. with teeth
3. without eyes
4. without hair
5. with a hat
6. with glasses
7. with teeth, without a nose
8. with a hat, without hair
9. without eyes, with glasses
10. with teeth, with a hat, and without hair

PAGE 34 3. A. Read the following sentences three times.

A. The paper clips are on the book.
B. The half sheet of paper is in the book.
C. The glasses are next to the book.
D. The map is above the book.
E. The pencil is between the two books.
F. The sheet of paper is under the book.
G. Two pens are to the left of the book and three pens are to the right of the book.
H. Three books are in front of Rosa.
I. Seven books are behind Paulo.

Chapter 3

LESSON 1

PAGE 36 1. A. Read the following three times.

A. Bill D. Bill's two brothers G. Bill's three children
B. Bill's father E. Bill's wife H. Bill's two daughters
C. Bill's mother F. Bill's sister I. Bill's son

PAGE 37 1. B. Read the following. The students write the corresponding letters on the lines provided.

1. Bill's mother
2. Bill
3. Bill's two brothers
4. Bill's three children
5. Bill's son
6. Bill's wife
7. Bill's two daughters
8. Bill's father
9. Bill's wife and Bill's sister
10. Bill's two brothers and Bill's son
11. Bill's two daughters, Bill's mother, and Bill's father
12. Bill's three children, Bill's sister, and Bill's wife

PAGE 37 1. C. Spell each word. The students write the words on the lines provided on page 36.

B. father F A T H E R father
C. mother M O T H E R mother
D. brothers B R O T H E R S brothers
E. wife W I F E wife
F. sister S I S T E R sister
G. children C H I L D R E N children
H. daughters D A U G H T E R S daughters
I. son S O N son

PAGE 37 1. E. Read the sentences of 1. D. The students write TRUE or FALSE on a sheet of paper.

PAGE 41 2. A. Read the following parts of the body three times.

A. head F. right foot
B. arms G. left foot
C. fingers H. toes
D. body I. right hand
E. legs J. left hand

PAGE 41 2. B. Read the following. The students write the corresponding letters on the lines provided.

1. fingers
2. legs
3. head
4. toes
5. body
6. arms and right foot
7. left hand, fingers, and toes
8. right hand, legs, and head

PAGE 41 2. C. Spell each word. The students write the words on the lines provided.

A. head H E A D head
B. arms A R M S arms
C. fingers F I N G E R S fingers
D. body B O D Y body
E. legs L E G S legs
F. right foot right R I G H T foot F O O T right foot
G. left foot left L E F T foot F O O T left foot
H. toes T O E S toes
I. right hand right R I G H T hand H A N D right hand
J. left hand left L E F T hand H A N D left hand

PAGE 42 3. A. Read the following sentences three times.

A. She doesn't have arms.
B. It doesn't have a nose.
C. She doesn't have a head.
D. He doesn't have a right foot.
E. They don't have noses.
F. They don't have right hands.
G. They don't have bodies.
H. She doesn't have ten fingers.
I. He doesn't have ten toes.

PAGE 42 3. B. Read the following sentences. The students write the corresponding letters on the lines provided.

1. She doesn't have a head.
2. He doesn't have a right foot.
3. It doesn't have a nose.
4. They don't have bodies.
5. She doesn't have ten fingers. He doesn't have ten toes.
6. They don't have noses. They don't have right hands.
7. She doesn't have a head. They don't have bodies.
8. It doesn't have a nose. They don't have noses.

LESSON 3

PAGE 44 1. A. Read the following three times.

A. Bill
B. his grandparents, George and Ida
C. his aunts, Grace and Nina
D. his parents, James and Mary
E. his uncle, Ron
F. his sister's husband, Pablo
G. his nephew, Steve
H. his niece, Laura.
I. his children's cousins, Steve and Laura

PAGE 45 1. B. Read the following. The students write the corresponding letters on the lines provided.

1. Bill
2. his parents
3. his sister's husband
4. his grandparents
5. his niece and his nephew
6. his aunts and his uncle
7. his grandparents, his parents, and his niece
8. his uncle, his sister's husband, and his children's cousins

PAGE 45 1. C. Spell each word. The students write the words on the lines provided.

B. grandparents G R A N D P A R E N T S grandparents
C. aunts A U N T S aunts
D. parents P A R E N T S parents
E. uncle U N C L E uncle
F. sister's husband sister's S I S T E R ' S husband H U S B A N D sister's husband
G. nephew N E P H E W nephew
H. niece N I E C E niece
I. cousins C O U S I N S cousins

PAGE 45 2. A. Divide the students into groups of four. Have them practice saying, "My name is . . .", "Your name is . . . ", etc.

LESSON 4

PAGE 49 1. C. Read the questions of 1. B. The students write a YES or NO sentence on a sheet of paper.

PAGE 50 2. A. Read the following passage. Tell the students that there are eleven words missing and instruct them to put a caret (∧) wherever there is a word missing.

Our uncle's wife *has* a Japanese father and a French mother. *Our* uncle *is* half Spanish and half British. He and his wife *have* six children. *Their* daughters *have* French and Japanese names and *their* sons *have* Spanish and British names. The children's grandparents *are* from four countries but *their* grandchildren *are* 100 percent American.

PAGE 50 3. A. Read the commands of 3. A. Model for the students as needed.

Chapter 4

LESSON 1

PAGE 52 1. A. Pointing to the compass, read the following three times.

A. north
B. northeast
C. east
D. southeast
E. south
F. southwest
G. west
H. northwest.

154 Back of the Book

PAGE 52 1. B. Spell each word. The students write the words on the lines provided.

A. north N O R T H north
B. northeast N O R T H E A S T northeast
C. east E A S T east
D. southeast S O U T H E A S T southeast
E. south S O U T H south
F. southwest S O U T H W E S T southwest
G. west W E S T west
H. northwest N O R T H W E S T northwest

PAGE 52 1. C. Tell the students to stand and face north. Read the following commands. Model for the students as needed.

Point north.
Point west.
Point east.
Point south.
Point northeast.
Point northwest.
Point southwest.
Point southeast.

PAGE 55 3. A. Read the following verbs three times.

A. eat
B. drink
C. sleep
D. wash
E. fly
F. swim
G. run
H. drive
I. cry

PAGE 55 3. B. Read the following. The students write the corresponding letters on the lines provided.

1. sleep
2. swim
3. wash
4. drink
5. run and swim
6. drive and fly
7. eat and drink
8. cry, sleep, and wash
9. run, swim, and fly

PAGE 55 3. C. Spell each word. The students write the words on the lines provided.

A. eat E A T eat
B. drink D R I N K drink
C. sleep S L E E P sleep
D. wash W A S H wash
E. fly F L Y fly
F. swim S W I M swim
G. run R U N run
H. drive D R I V E drive
I. cry C R Y cry

LESSON 2

PAGE 56 1. A. Read the following adjectives three times.

A. happy
B. sad
C. hungry
D. thirsty
E. tired
F. dirty
G. clean

PAGE 56 1. B. Read the following. The students write the corresponding letters on the lines provided.

1. sad
2. thirsty
3. happy
4. clean
5. tired
6. thirsty and hungry
7. sad and happy
8. dirty and clean
9. tired, hungry, and sad

PAGE 56 1. C. Spell each word. The students write the words on the lines provided.

A. happy H A P P Y happy
B. sad S A D sad
C. hungry H U N G R Y hungry
D. thirsty T H I R S T Y thirsty
E. tired T I R E D tired
F. dirty D I R T Y dirty
G. clean C L E A N clean

PAGE 58 3. A. Read the following three times.

A. people
B. insects
C. animals
D. apple
E. banana
F. pizza

PAGE 58 3. B. Read the following. The students write the corresponding letters on the lines provided.

1. insects
2. banana
3. apple and pizza
4. people and animals
5. insects, apple, and banana
6. pizza, animals, and people

PAGE 58 3. C. Spell each word. The students write the words on the lines provided.

A. people P E O P L E people
B. insects I N S E C T S insects
C. animals A N I M A L S animals
D. apple A P P L E apple
E. banana B A N A N A banana
F. pizza P I Z Z A pizza

LESSON 3

PAGE 60 1. A. Read the following three times.

A. gloves
B. jacket
C. shirt
D. belt
E. pants
F. shoes
G. suit
H. necktie
I. blouse
J. skirt
K. sandals
L. dress

Instructions, Tapescripts **155**

PAGE 60 1. B. Read the following. The students write the corresponding letters on the lines provided.

1. dress
2. jacket
3. pants
4. blouse
5. shoes and sandals
6. shirt and pants
7. jacket and gloves
8. blouse and skirt
9. suit, shirt, and necktie
10. skirt, blouse, and dress
11. shirt, belt, and pants
12. shoes, sandals, gloves, and jacket

PAGE 60 1. C. Spell each word. The students write the words on the lines provided.

A. shirt S H I R T shirt
B. belt B E L T belt
C. pants P A N T S pants
D. shoes S H O E S shoes
E. jacket J A C K E T jacket
F. gloves G L O V E S gloves
G. suit S U I T suit
H. necktie N E C K T I E necktie
I. blouse B L O U S E blouse
J. skirt S K I R T skirt
K. sandals S A N D A L S sandals
L. dress D R E S S dress

PAGE 61 2. A. Tell the students to look at the back cover. Say the following colors three times.

1. red
2. blue
3. black
4. green
5. yellow
6. white
7. brown
8. orange
9. pink
10. grey
11. tan
12. purple

PAGE 62 3. A. Read the following verbs three times.

A. wave
B. clap
C. stand up
D. sit down
E. write
F. point
G. listen
H. think
I. read

PAGE 62 3. B. Spell each word. The students write the words on the lines provided.

A. wave W A V E wave
B. clap C L A P clap
C. stand up stand S T A N D up U P stand up
D. sit down sit S I T down D O W N sit down
E. write W R I T E write
F. point P O I N T point
G. listen L I S T E N listen
H. think T H I N K think
I. read R E A D read

PAGE 62 3. C. Read the following commands. Have the students perform each command. Model for them if needed.

clap
wave
point
stand up
sit down and think
read and write
point, wave, and listen
stand up, clap, wave, and sit down

LESSON 4

PAGE 64 1. A. Read the following sentences three times.

A. They're playing soccer.
B. They're playing tennis.
C. They're playing baseball.
D. They're playing golf.
E. They're playing basketball.
F. They're playing volleyball.

PAGE 64 1. B. Read the following sentences. The students write the corresponding letters on the lines provided.

1. They're playing basketball.
2. They're playing golf.
3. They're playing volleyball.
4. They're playing tennis.
5. They're playing baseball and they're playing soccer.
6. They're playing tennis and they're playing golf.
7. They're playing baseball, they're playing volleyball, and they're playing golf.
8. They're playing basketball, they're playing tennis, and they're playing soccer.

PAGE 64 1. C. Spell each word. The students write the words on the lines provided.

A. They're playing soccer. soccer S O C C E R soccer
B. They're playing tennis. tennis T E N N I S tennis
C. They're playing baseball. baseball B A S E B A L L baseball
D. They're playing golf. golf G O L F golf
E. They're playing basketball. basketball B A S K E T B A L L basketball
F. They're playing volleyball. Volleyball V O L L E Y B A L L volleyball

PAGE 65 2. A. Read the following sentences three times.

A. Bill is going to play basketball.
B. Bill is playing basketball.
C. Bill is going to play tennis.
D. Bill is playing tennis.
E. Bill is going to play soccer.
F. Bill is playing soccer.
G. Bill is going to play baseball.
H. Bill is playing baseball.
I. Bill is going to play volleyball.
J. Bill is playing volleyball.
K. Bill is going to play golf.
L. Bill is playing golf.

Back of the Book

PAGE 66 4. A. Read the following dialog. Tell the students that there are fifteen words missing and instruct them to put a caret (∧) wherever there is a word missing.

Miguel: My sister *is* going to go to Hawaii.
Rosa: Hawaii? How wonderful! When is she going *to* go?
Miguel: Tomorrow. She's going to be *in* Hawaii *for* two weeks. She's going to *swim* and *play* golf every day.
Rosa: *Are* you going to go to Hawaii?
Miguel: No, I'm *going* to go to Chicago. It's January and *I'm* going to go to a cold city.
Rosa: Don't *be* sad. Chicago is *a* wonderful city.
Miguel: Not *in* January. I am going to wear a jacket and gloves *in* Chicago and my *sister* is going to wear sandals *and* a T-shirt in Hawaii.

Chapter 5
LESSON 1

PAGE 68 1. A. Read the following times three times.

A. two o'clock
B. seven o'clock
C. four ten
D. one fifteen
E. five twenty
F. twelve thirty
G. ten forty
H. eight forty-five
I. twelve noon
J. twelve midnight

PAGE 68 1. B. Read the following times. The students write the corresponding letters on the lines provided.

1. five twenty
2. seven o'clock
3. four ten
4. two o'clock and one fifteen
5. eight forty five and twelve thirty
6. ten forty and twelve noon
7. five twenty, twelve midnight, and two o'clock
8. one fifteen, four ten, and seven o'clock
9. twelve noon, ten forty, and twelve thirty

PAGE 69 2. B. Read the questions of 2. A. The students write YES or NO on a sheet of paper.

PAGE 70 3. A. Read the descriptions for each of the pictures three times, stressing that this is what will happen "tomorrow."

A. At 7:30 Bill will get up.
B. At 7:35 Bill will eat breakfast.
C. At 8:00 Bill will shave.
D. At 8:15 Bill will brush his teeth.
E. At 8:20 Bill will shower.
F. At 8:30 Bill will get dressed.
G. At 8:45 Bill will leave his house.
H. At 9:45 Bill will arrive at the airport.
I. At 10:15 Bill will check in.
J. At 11:20 Bill will board the airplane.
K. At 11:55 Bill will take off.

PAGE 70 3. B. Read the following. The students write the corresponding letters on the lines provided.

1. Bill will eat breakfast.
2. Bill will get up.
3. Bill will shave and he will shower.
4. Bill will get dressed and he will leave his house.
5. Bill will board the airplane and he will take off.
6. Bill will leave his house, he will arrive at the airport, and he will check in.
7. Bill will shave, he will brush his teeth, and he will get dressed.

PAGE 70 3. C. Spell each word. The students write the words on the lines provided.

A. get up get G E T up U P get up
B. eat breakfast eat E A T eat breakfast
C. shave S H A V E shave
D. brush his teeth brush B R U S H brush his teeth
E. shower S H O W E R shower
F. get dressed get G E T dressed D R E S S E D get dressed
G. leave his house leave L E A V E leave his house
H. arrive at the airport arrive A R R I V E arrive at the airport
I. check in check C H E C K in I N check in
J. board the airplane board B O A R D board the airplane
K. take off take T A K E off O F F take off

PAGE 71 4. B. Read the questions of 4. A. The students write YES or NO on a sheet of paper.

LESSON 2

PAGE 72 1. A. Pointing to the calendar, say the months of the year three times.

January	May	September
February	June	October
March	July	November
April	August	December

Instructions, Tapescripts **157**

PAGE 72 1. B. Spell each month. The students write the months on a sheet of paper.

January J A N U A R Y January	July J U L Y July
February F E B R U A R Y February	August A U G U S T August
March M A R C H March	September S E P T E M B E R September
April A P R I L April	October O C T O B E R October
May M A Y May	November N O V E M B E R November
June J U N E June	December D E C E M B E R December

PAGE 73 1. D. Read the questions of 1. C. The students write YES or NO on a sheet of paper.

PAGE 74 2. A. Pointing to the calendar on pages 74-75, say the following three times.

January is the first month.	July is the seventh month.
February is the second month.	August is the eighth month.
March is the third month.	September is the ninth month.
April is the fourth month.	October is the tenth month.
May is the fifth month.	November is the eleventh month.
June is the sixth month.	December is the twelfth month.

PAGE 75 2. C. Read the questions of 2. B. The students write the months on a sheet of paper.

PAGE 75 3. A. Read the list of holidays three times.

A. New Year's Day	E. Father's Day
B. Lincoln's Birthday	F. Labor Day
C. Mother's Day	G. Thanksgiving
D. Memorial Day	H. Christmas

PAGE 75 3. B. Read the following list of holidays. The students write the corresponding letters on the lines provided.

1. Mother's Day	5. Father's Day and Mother's Day
2. Thanksgiving	6. Lincoln's Birthday and Christmas
3. New Year's Day	7. Labor Day and Memorial Day
4. Memorial Day	8. New Year's Day, Thanksgiving, and Christmas

PAGE 75 3. C. Spell each word. The students write the words on the lines provided.

A. New Year's Day new N E W year's Y E A R' S day D A Y New Year's Day
B. Lincoln's Birthday Lincoln's L I N C O L N' S birthday B I R T H D A Y Lincoln's Birthday
C. Mother's Day mother's M O T H E R' S day D A Y Mother's Day
D. Memorial Day memorial M E M O R I A L day D A Y Memorial Day
E. Father's Day father's F A T H E R' S day D A Y Father's Day
F. Labor Day labor L A B O R day D A Y Labor Day
G. Thanksgiving T H A N K S G I V I N G Thanksgiving
H. Christmas C H R I S T M A S Christmas

PAGE 79 3. A. Read the following passage. Tell the students that there are sixteen words missing, and instruct them to put a caret (∧) wherever there is a word missing.

Some day I will be rich! First, *I'll* buy *my* mother and father a new house. Second, *I'll* give my sister *all* the money *she'll* need to go to *the* university. Some day *she'll* be a doctor and *my* parents *will* be very happy. Third, *my* wife and *I* will fly around the world. *We'll* fly to Paris, Madrid, Cairo, Bangkok, Hong Kong, Tokyo, *and* San Francisco. Finally, *we'll* buy a house *in* California and *we'll* have a big family.

Chapter 6: Review

PAGE 83 5. A. Read the following dialog. Tell the students that there are twenty words missing and instruct them to put in a caret (∧) wherever there is a word missing.

Rita: Isabel, what *are* you doing?
Isabel: *I'm* writing to my daughter.
Rita: Your daughter *in* Colombia?
Isabel: No, *my* daughter in Canada.
Rita: Oh, you *have* a daughter in Canada?
Isabel: Yes, there *is* a photograph of her *on* the wall.
Rita: But there are *two* photos. Is *she* on the *right* or on the left?
Isabel: On the left. *She's* wearing a jacket and gloves.

158 Back of the Book

Rita: *Who* are the *children* in the photo on the right?
Isabel: They are my *niece* and nephew.
Rita: *They're* wearing sun glasses and sandals and they are very *happy*.
Isabel: Yes, they're in Mexico *with* my parents. They go *to* Mexico in January and *February* because it *isn't* cold.

Chapter 7
LESSON 1

PAGE 84 1. A. Read the following parts of the body three times.

A. shoulder
B. elbow
C. wrist
D. stomach
E. knee
F. ankle
G. chin
H. neck

PAGE 84 1. B. Read the following. The students write the corresponding letters on the lines provided.

1. knee
2. shoulder
3. stomach
4. wrist
5. elbow and knee
6. shoulder and wrist
7. knee and ankle
8. chin, neck, and stomach
9. wrist, elbow, and shoulder

PAGE 84 1. C. Spell each word. The students write the words on the lines provided.

A. shoulder S H O U L D E R shoulder
B. elbow E L B O W elbow
C. wrist W R I S T wrist
D. stomach S T O M A C H stomach
E. knee K N E E knee
F. ankle A N K L E ankle
G. chin C H I N chin
H. neck N E C K neck

PAGE 86 3. A. Read the actions. Have the students perform each action. Model for them if needed.

PAGE 87 5. A. Read the following words three times.

A. chickens
B. ducks
C. dogs
D. cats
E. horses
F. fish
G. spiders
H. bees
I. snakes
J. monkeys
K. birds
L. sheep

PAGE 87 5. B. Read the following. The students write the corresponding letters on the lines provided.

1. snakes
2. fish
3. bees and spiders
4. birds, cats, and dogs
5. horses, sheep, and monkeys
6. ducks, chickens, and birds
7. spiders, bees, and fish
8. dogs, chickens, and horses
9. ducks, cats, and sheep

PAGE 87 5. C. Spell each word. The students write the words on the lines provided.

A. chickens C H I C K E N S chickens
B. ducks D U C K S ducks
C. dogs D O G S dogs
D. cats C A T S cats
E. horses H O R S E S horses
F. fish F I S H fish
G. spiders S P I D E R S spiders
H. bees B E E S bees
I. snakes S N A K E S snakes
J. monkeys M O N K E Y S monkeys
K. birds B I R D S birds
L. sheep S H E E P sheep

LESSON 2

PAGE 88 1. B. Read the questions of 1. A. The students write "Yes, they can." or "No, they can't." on a sheet of paper.

PAGE 90 3. A. Read the following words three times.

A. piano
B. guitar
C. drums
D. harmonica
E. dominos
F. checkers
G. chess
H. Ping-Pong

PAGE 90 3. B. Read the following. The students write the corresponding letters on the lines provided.

1. drums
2. Ping-Pong
3. guitar and harmonica
4. piano and dominos
5. checkers and chess
6. Ping-Pong and dominos
7. guitar, piano, and checkers
8. chess, harmonica, and drums

PAGE 90 3. C. Spell each word. The students write the words on the lines provided.

A. piano P I A N O piano
B. guitar G U I T A R guitar
C. drums D R U M S drums
D. harmonica H A R M O N I C A harmonica
E. dominos D O M I N O S dominos
F. checkers C H E C K E R S checkers
G. chess C H E S S chess
H. Ping-Pong P I N G - P O N G Ping-Pong

LESSON 3

PAGE 92 1. A. Read the following words three times.

A. tennis racket
B. baseball and bat
C. fishing pole
D. golf clubs
E. skis
F. skates
G. soccer ball
H. football
I. paddle

PAGE 92 1. B. Read the following. The students write the corresponding letters on the lines provided.

1. baseball and bat
2. soccer ball
3. skates and skis
4. tennis racket and fishing pole
5. football and golf clubs
6. fishing pole, paddle, and skates
7. soccer ball, tennis racket, and skis
8. golf clubs, football, paddle, and baseball and bat

PAGE 92 1. C. Spell each word. The students write the words on the lines provided.

A. tennis racket, tennis T E N N I S racket R A C K E T tennis racket
B. baseball and bat, baseball B A S E B A L L and A N D bat B A T baseball and bat
C. fishing pole, fishing F I S H I N G pole P O L E fishing pole
D. golf clubs, golf G O L F clubs C L U B S golf clubs
E. skis S K I S skis
F. skates S K A T E S skates
G. soccer ball, soccer S O C C E R ball B A L L soccer ball
H. football F O O T B A L L football
I. paddle P A D D L E paddle

PAGE 94 3. A. Read each of the following sentences three times.

1. They don't have fishing poles. They won't be able to fish.
2. He doesn't have a tennis racket. He won't be able to play tennis.
3. She doesn't have golf clubs. She won't be able to play golf.
4. He doesn't have a bat. He won't be able to play baseball.
5. They don't have a soccer ball. They won't be able to play soccer.
6. They don't have a basketball. They won't be able to play basketball.
7. He doesn't have skates. He won't be able to play hockey.
8. They don't have paddles. They won't be able to play Ping-Pong.

PAGE 95 4. A. Read the following dialog. Tell the students that there are eighteen words missing, and instruct them to put a caret (∧) wherever there is a word missing.

Jenny: Hi, Lydia, *what* are you doing?
Lydia: *I'm* reading a book.
Jenny: *Can* you play tennis?
Lydia: No, I *don't* have my racket.
Jenny: Who has *it*?
Lydia: Julie has *it*, and she and her mother *will* be in Chicago today and tomorrow.
Jenny: *Will* you play tennis *with* me tomorrow?
Lydia: No, I *can't* tomorrow, but I will *be* able *to* play on Tuesday.
Jenny: No, you *won't* be able *to* play tennis on Tuesday.
Lydia: *Why* not?
Jenny: Because Julie *is* going *to* play tennis with me on Tuesday, and she *will* have your racket.

Chapter 8

LESSON 1

PAGE 96 1. A. Read the following three times.

A. square
B. rectangle
C. triangle
D. circle
E. oval
F. line
G. star
H. arrow

PAGE 96 1. B. Read the following. The students write the corresponding letters on the lines provided.

1. circle
2. star
3. square
4. arrow
5. oval and rectangle
6. triangle and line
7. circle and square
8. arrow, oval, and star
9. rectangle, triangle, and line

160   Back of the Book

PAGE 96 1. C. Spell each word. The students write the words on the lines provided.

A. square S Q U A R E square
B. rectangle R E C T A N G L E rectangle
C. triangle T R I A N G L E triangle
D. circle C I R C L E circle

E. oval O V A L oval
F. line L I N E line
G. star S T A R star
H. arrow A R R O W arrow

PAGE 97 2. A. Read the commands. Have the students perform each command. Model for them if needed.

PAGE 97 2. B. Read the following questions. The students write YES or NO on a sheet of paper.

1. Is the square in the circle?
2. Is the rectangle to the right of the square?
3. Are the stars under the square?
4. Is the oval in the rectangle?
5. Are the arrows above the lines?
6. Is the square between the rectangle and the triangle?
7. Are the lines under the rectangle?
8. Is the triangle next to the square?
9. Are the lines between the rectangle and the arrows?

PAGE 98 3. A. Ask a student to come to the front of the classroom, and give the student the directions listed here. Have a table, book, two pencils, two sheets of paper, and a half sheet of paper ready. Have the student keep his or her back to the class.

Put the book on the table.
Put the half sheet of paper in the book.
Put a pencil to the right of the book.

Put the two sheets of paper under the book.
Put a pencil to the left of the book.

Then ask another student to come to the front of the classroom and follow the directions listed here.

Take away the pencil on the right.
Take away the half sheet of paper.
Take away the pencil on the left.

Take away the two sheets of paper.
Take away the book.

PAGE 98 3. C. Read the questions of 3. B. The students write YES or NO on a sheet of paper.

LESSON 2

PAGE 99 1. A. Read the descriptions for each of the pictures three times.

A. Rosa's at home.
B. She's at school.
C. She's at work.
D. She's at the supermarket.
E. She's at the mall.
F. She's at the movies.
G. She's at the library.
H. She's at the gym.

PAGE 99 1. B. Read the following. The students write the corresponding letters on the lines provided.

1. Rosa's at the movies.
2. She's at school.
3. She's at the mall.
4. She's at work and she's at the gym.
5. She's at home and she's at the library.
6. She's at the supermarket and she's at the movies.
7. She's at home, at the gym, and at the supermarket.
8. She's at the mall, at the library, and at work.

PAGE 99 1. C. Spell each word. The students write the words on the lines provided.

A. home H O M E home
B. school S C H O O L school
C. work W O R K work
D. supermarket S U P E R M A R K E T supermarket

E. mall M A L L mall
F. movies M O V I E S movies
G. library L I B R A R Y library
H. gym G Y M gym

PAGE 102 4. A. Read the following three times.

A. baseball player
B. golfer
C. fisherman
D. tennis player
E. hockey player
F. soccer player
G. basketball player
H. boxer
I. volleyball player

PAGE 102 4. B. Read the following. The students write the corresponding letters on the lines provided.

1. boxer
2. hockey player and tennis player
3. volleyball player and fisherman
4. soccer player and basketball player
5. golfer and baseball player
6. boxer, fisherman, and golfer

Instructions, Tapescripts **161**

PAGE 102 4. C. Spell each word. The students write the words on the lines provided.

A. baseball player, baseball B A S E B A L L player P L A Y E R baseball player
B. golfer G O L F E R golfer
C. fisherman F I S H E R M A N fisherman
D. tennis player, tennis T E N N I S player P L A Y E R tennis player
E. hockey player, hockey H O C K E Y player P L A Y E R hockey player
F. soccer player, soccer S O C C E R player P L A Y E R soccer player
G. basketball player, basketball B A S K E T B A L L player P L A Y E R basketball player
H. boxer B O X E R boxer
I. volleyball player, volleyball V O L L E Y B A L L player P L A Y E R volleyball player

PAGE 103 5. B. Read the sentences of 5. A. The students write TRUE or FALSE on a sheet of paper.

LESSON 3

PAGE 104 1. A. Read the following three times.

A. broom
B. pen
C. razor
D. brush
E. needle
F. car
G. spade
H. horse
I. scissors
J. chair

PAGE 104 1. B. Read the following. The students write the corresponding letters on the lines provided.

1. pen
2. needle
3. chair
4. scissors and spade
5. razor and brush
6. broom and car
7. razor, scissors, and needle
8. broom, brush, and spade
9. car, chair, and horse
10. spade, razor, and pen

PAGE 104 1. C. Spell each word. The students write the words on the lines provided.

A. broom B R O O M broom
B. pen P E N pen
C. razor R A Z O R razor
D. brush B R U S H brush
E. needle N E E D L E needle
F. car C A R car
G. spade S P A D E spade
H. horse H O R S E horse
I. scissors S C I S S O R S scissors
J. chair C H A I R chair

PAGE 105 2. A. Read the following three times.

A. sweep
B. write
C. shave
D. paint
E. sew
F. drive
G. dig
H. ride
I. cut
J. sit

PAGE 105 2. B. Read the following. The students write the corresponding letters on the lines provided.

1. paint
2. sit
3. cut
4. sweep and drive
5. dig and sew
6. write and shave
7. sew, sweep, and dig
8. ride, drive, and sit
9. paint, write, and cut
10. shave, dig, and drive

PAGE 105 2. C. Spell each word. The students write the words on the lines provided.

A. sweep S W E E P sweep
B. write W R I T E write
C. shave S H A V E shave
D. paint P A I N T paint
E. sew S E W sew
F. drive D R I V E drive
G. dig D I G dig
H. ride R I D E ride
I. cut C U T cut
J. sit S I T sit

162 Back of the Book

PAGE 107 4. A. Read the following passage. Tell the students that there are twenty-five words missing and instruct them to put a caret (∧) wherever there is a word missing.

Our family lives *in* Toronto, but my parents are *from* Mexico. In Mexico my father *was* a teacher, and my mother *was* a nurse. They *weren't* rich, but they *weren't* poor. Here in Canada *my* father teaches Spanish, and *my* mother works *in* a library. There *are* three children in our family. I'm 17 years old; my sister is *15;* and my brother *is* 10.

My father and mother *were* happy when they *were* in Mexico. But here *in* Toronto my father has more money. *They* like Canada, but they *don't* like the weather. My father always says, "In Mexico it *was* always warm."

My grandmother *didn't* go with us to Canada. She *wasn't* happy to see our family go to Toronto. She wants us to return *to* Mexico. *My* father and mother want to return, but my sister, my brother, and I *don't* want to return. We *are* Canadians. *We* want to stay here.

Chapter 9

LESSON 1

PAGE 109 2. A. Read the following three times.

A. letter
B. potatoes
C. television
D. radio
E. baby
F. mail
G. receive
H. cook
I. watch
J. listen
K. kiss

PAGE 109 2. B. Read the following. The students write the words on the lines provided.

1. baby
2. potatoes
3. letter
4. radio and television
5. watch and listen
6. receive and mail
7. kiss, cook, and listen
8. potatoes, baby, and letter
9. mail, receive, listen, and watch
10. cook, potatoes, kiss, baby

PAGE 109 2.C. Spell each word. The students write the words on the lines provided.

A. letter L E T T E R letter
B. potatoes P O T A T O E S potatoes
C. television T E L E V I S I O N television
D. radio R A D I O radio
E. baby B A B Y baby
F. mail M A I L mail
G. receive R E C E I V E receive
H. cook C O O K cook
I. watch W A T C H watch
J. listen L I S T E N listen
K. kiss K I S S kiss

PAGE 111 5. B. Read the questions of 5. A. The students write *Yes, I did* or *No, I didn't* on a sheet of paper.

LESSON 2

PAGE 112 1. A. Read the following words three times.

A. computer
B. camera
C. microwave
D. newspaper
E. telephone
F. e-mail
G. candle
H. light bulb
I. contact lens

PAGE 112 1. B. Read the following. The students write the corresponding letters on the lines provided.

1. camera
2. telephone
3. microwave
4. newspaper and computer
5. light bulb and candle
6. contact lens, camera, and computer
7. e-mail, newspaper, and telephone
8. microwave, contact lens, and e-mail

PAGE 112 1. C. Spell each word. The students write the words on the lines provided. Teach the word *hyphen* for item F.

A. computer C O M P U T E R computer
B. camera C A M E R A camera
C. microwave M I C R O W A V E microwave
D. newspaper N E W S P A P E R newspaper
E. telephone T E L E P H O N E telephone
F. e-mail E - M A I L e-mail
G. candle C A N D L E candle
H. light bulb, light L I G H T bulb B U L B light bulb
I. contact lens, contact C O N T A C T lens L E N S contact lens

Instructions, Tapescripts **163**

PAGE 114 4. A. Read the following words three times.

A. hot
B. warm
C. cool
D. cold
E. sunny
F. rainy
G. cloudy
H. windy
I. snowy

PAGE 114 4. B. Read the following. The students write the corresponding letters on the lines provided.

1. cool
2. sunny
3. rainy and cloudy
4. hot and warm
5. cold and snowy
6. windy, rainy, and snowy
7. cloudy, sunny, and windy
8. hot, cold, warm, and cool

PAGE 114 4. C. Spell each word. The students write the words on the lines provided.

A. hot H O T hot
B. warm W A R M warm
C. cool C O O L cool
D. cold C O L D cold
E. sunny S U N N Y sunny
F. rainy R A I N Y rainy
G. cloudy C L O U D Y cloudy
H. windy W I N D Y windy
I. snowy S N O W Y snowy

LESSON 3

PAGE 116 1. A. Read the following words three times.

A. clothes
B. suitcase
C. elephant
D. turtle
E. mouse
F. temperature
G. summer
H. fall
I. winter
J. spring

PAGE 116 1. B. Read the following. The students write the corresponding letters on the lines provided.

1. mouse
2. clothes
3. temperature
4. spring and fall
5. elephant and turtle
6. suitcase and clothes
7. winter and summer
8. turtle, mouse, and elephant
9. temperature, clothes, and suitcase
10. winter, spring, summer, and fall

PAGE 116 1. C. Spell each word. The students write the words on the lines provided.

A. clothes C L O T H E S clothes
B. suitcase S U I T C A S E suitcase
C. elephant E L E P H A N T elephant
D. turtle T U R T L E turtle
E. mouse M O U S E mouse
F. temperature T E M P E R A T U R E temperature
G. summer S U M M E R summer
H. fall F A L L fall
I. winter W I N T E R winter
J. spring S P R I N G spring

PAGE 117 2. A. Read the following words three times.

A. old
B. young
C. tall
D. short
E. heavy
F. light
G. high
H. low
I. old
J. new
K. big
L. little
M. fast
N. slow
O. long
P. short

PAGE 117 2. B. Read the following. The students write the corresponding letters on the lines provided.

1. tall
2. fast
3. heavy
4. old and young
5. high and low
6. heavy and light
7. long and short
8. new and old
9. big, little, and slow
10. fast, long, young, and new

PAGE 117 2. C. Spell each word. The students write the words on the lines provided.

A. old O L D old
B. young Y O U N G young
C. tall T A L L tall
D. short S H O R T short
E. heavy H E A V Y heavy
F. light L I G H T light
G. high H I G H high
H. low L O W low
I. old O L D old
J. new N E W new
K. big B I G big
L. little L I T T L E little
M. fast F A S T fast
N. slow S L O W slow
O. long L O N G long
P. short S H O R T short

Back of the Book

PAGE 119 5. B. Read the following dialog. Tell the students that there are twenty-one words missing and instruct them to put a caret (∧) wherever there is a word missing.

Anna: Grandmother, when *were* you born?
Grandmother: I *was* born in 1921.
Anna: *Did* you watch a lot of television when you *were* a girl?
Grandmother: No, people didn't *have* televisions. They listened *to* the radio.
Anna: *Did* people have cars?
Grandmother: Oh, yes, there *were* a lot of cars. My family had an old black car.
Anna: How about *computers*? Did you *have* a computer?
Grandmother: No, there *weren't* any computers. We didn't *have* video games like you *have* today.
Anna: What about movies? *Did* you go to the movies?
Grandmother: Oh, yes, there *were* movies, but they *weren't* in color.
Anna: No color! *Didn't* they have color?
Grandmother: No, they *didn't*. It *was* all black and white.
Anna: Movies *without* color! Grandmother, is that *true*?

Chapter 10

LESSON 1

PAGE 120 1. A. Read the following numbers three times. (One billion is 1,000,000,000,000 in British usage.)

A. one hundred
B. one thousand
C. ten thousand
D. twenty thousand
E. one hundred thousand
F. one million
G. ten million
H. one hundred million
I. one billion

PAGE 120 1. B. Read the following numbers. The students write the corresponding letters on the lines provided.

1. one thousand
2. one million
3. twenty thousand
4. one million and one billion
5. ten thousand and ten million
6. one hundred, one hundred thousand, and one hundred million

PAGE 120 2. A. Read the following numbers. The students circle the numbers read.

1. one thousand one hundred eighty-nine
2. thirty-four thousand four hundred forty-seven
3. one hundred six thousand
4. five hundred eight thousand two hundred
5. seven hundred twenty-four thousand three hundred fifty
6. one million two hundred ninety-eight thousand
7. eleven million one hundred forty-one thousand
8. three hundred million eight hundred sixty-three thousand
9. four billion five hundred forty million
10. sixty-two billion four hundred eighty million seven hundred forty-two thousand

PAGE 121 2. C. Read the following numbers. The students write the numbers on the lines provided.

1. nine million three hundred sixty-three thousand
2. two million nine hundred forty-two thousand
3. four million fifty-seven thousand
4. six million eight hundred eighty-six thousand
5. twenty-eight million three hundred ninety-five thousand
6. seventy million five hundred forty thousand
7. ninety-four million thirty-five thousand
8. one hundred eleven million seven hundred seven thousand
9. three billion six hundred sixty-four million eight hundred twelve thousand
10. twelve billion four hundred thirty-three million two hundred twenty-three thousand

PAGE 122 3. A. Read the following three times.

A. Pacific Ocean
B. Atlantic Ocean
C. Indian Ocean
D. Arctic Ocean
E. Europe
F. Africa
G. Asia
H. North America
I. South America
J. Australia

PAGE 122 3. B. Read the following. The students write the corresponding letters on the lines provided.
1. Arctic Ocean
2. Pacific Ocean
3. Atlantic Ocean and Indian Ocean
4. North America and South America
5. Europe and Africa
6. Asia, Australia, and Africa
7. Pacific Ocean, Atlantic Ocean, and Indian Ocean
8. Australia, North America, and Asia
9. Africa, Europe, Asia, and South America
10. Arctic Ocean, Indian Ocean, Atlantic Ocean, and Pacific Ocean

PAGE 122 3. C. Spell each word. The students write the words on the lines provided.
A. Pacific Ocean, Pacific P A C I F I C Ocean O C E A N Pacific Ocean
B. Atlantic Ocean, Atlantic A T L A N T I C Ocean O C E A N Atlantic Ocean
C. Indian Ocean, Indian I N D I A N Ocean O C E A N Indian Ocean
D. Arctic Ocean, Arctic A R C T I C Ocean O C E A N Arctic Ocean
E. Europe E U R O P E Europe
F. Africa A F R I C A Africa
G. Asia A S I A Asia
H. North America, North N O R T H America A M E R I C A North America
I. South America, South S O U T H America A M E R I C A South America
J. Australia A U S T R A L I A Australia

Then, pointing to the map, read the following list of places with their square mileage three times.
A. Pacific Ocean—sixty-four million one hundred eighty-six thousand square miles
B. Atlantic Ocean—thirty-one million five hundred thirty thousand square miles
C. Indian Ocean—twenty-eight million three hundred fifty-seven thousand square miles
D. Arctic Ocean—five million five hundred forty thousand square miles
E. Europe—four million fifty-seven thousand square miles
F. Africa—eleven million seven hundred seven thousand square miles
G. Asia—seventeen million one hundred twenty-nine thousand square miles
H. North America—nine million three hundred sixty-three thousand square miles
I. South America—six million eight hundred seventy-five thousand square miles
J. Australia—two million nine hundred sixty-six thousand square miles

LESSON 2

PAGE 124 1. A. Read the following three times.

A. boys
B. girls
C. motorcycle
D. bicycle
E. train
F. truck
G. cow
H. deer
I. rabbit
J. eggs
K. milk

PAGE 124 1. B. Read the following. The students write the corresponding letters on the lines provided.
1. bicycle
2. girls
3. eggs and milk
4. train and truck
5. deer and cow
6. boys and girls
7. rabbit and motorcycle
8. boys, eggs, and milk
9. cow, rabbit, and deer
10. truck, train, motorcycle, and bicycle

PAGE 124 1. C. Spell each word. The students write the words on the lines provided.
A. boys B O Y S boys
B. girls G I R L S girls
C. motorcycle M O T O R C Y C L E motorcycle
D. bicycle B I C Y C L E bicycle
E. train T R A I N train
F. truck T R U C K truck
G. cow C O W cow
H. deer D E E R deer
I. rabbit R A B B I T rabbit
J. eggs E G G S eggs
K. milk M I L K milk

PAGE 125 2. B. Read the questions of 2. A. The students write YES or NO on a sheet of paper.

PAGE 127 6. A. Read the following three times.

A. a penny, one cent
B. a nickel, five cents
C. a dime, ten cents
D. a quarter, twenty-five cents
E. a dollar, one hundred cents

PAGE 127 6. B. Read the following. The students write the letters on the lines provided.

1. a dime
2. a nickel
3. a penny and a quarter
4. a dime and a dollar
5. a penny, a nickel, and a quarter
6. a dollar, a nickel, and a dime
7. a penny, a quarter, a dollar, and a dime
8. a dollar, a quarter, a dime, a nickel, and a penny

LESSON 3

PAGE 128 1. A. Read each of the following sentences three times, pointing to the pictures and labels.

A. One thousand is more than one hundred.
B. A pound is less than a kilo.
C. An ounce is more than a gram.
D. A quart is less than a liter.
E. A gallon is more than two liters.
F. A dozen is more than ten.
G. A penny is less than a nickel.
H. A quarter is more than a dime.
I. A tablespoon is more than a teaspoon.
J. A cup is less than a pint.

PAGE 130 3. A. Pointing to the map, read the following cities and their populations three times.

Los Angeles has three million six hundred ninety-four thousand people.
Mexico City has eight million five hundred ninety-one thousand people.
Bogota has six million seven hundred twelve thousand people.
Chicago has two million eight hundred ninety-six thousand people.
Toronto has two million three hundred eighty-five thousand people.
Montreal has one million thirty-six thousand people.
New York has eight million eight thousand people.
Rio de Janeiro has five million eight hundred fifty thousand people.
Cairo has six million seven hundred eighty-nine thousand people.
Beijing has seven million three hundred sixty-two thousand people.
Seoul has ten million three hundred ten thousand people.
Tokyo has eight million one hundred thirty thousand people.

PAGE 131 5. A. Read the following passage. Tell the students that there are twenty-five words missing and instruct them to put a caret (∧) wherever there is a word missing.

When I was 16, *my* sister was 14. She was one year 11 months *younger* than I was. We *played* basketball and soccer. My sister was *taller* than the other players. She *had* long arms and long legs. I was *shorter* than the other players, and I had *short* arms and short legs. My sister was a very *good* basketball player, but I *wasn't*. From March to May *we* played soccer. My legs were *short*, but I was *fast*. I was faster *than* the tall girls. I was a *good* soccer player, but my sister *wasn't*.

Today I *have* two daughters. One plays basketball, *and* one plays soccer. My sister and I watch my *daughters* when they play, and we are *happy*. We *think* of the days when we were *young* and played basketball and soccer. One of my daughters is *tall*, and one is *short*. But the *taller* one is good at soccer, and the *shorter* one is good at basketball.

Chapter 11

LESSON 1

PAGE 134 2. A. Read the following words three times.

A. the planets
B. microbes
C. stars
D. the moon
E. the sun
F. mountains
G. telescope
H. microscope
I. night
J. day

PAGE 134 2. B. Read the following. The students write the corresponding letters on the lines provided.

1. night
2. mountains
3. the moon and stars
4. telescope and the planets
5. microscope, day, and the sun
6. microbes, mountains, and stars
7. the sun, the moon, microscope, and day
8. night, microbes, the planets, and telescope

Instructions, Tapescripts **167**

PAGE 134 2. C. Spell each word. The students write the words on the lines provided.

A. planets P L A N E T S planets
B. microbes M I C R O B E S microbes
C. stars S T A R S stars
D. moon M O O N moon
E. sun S U N sun
F. mountains M O U N T A I N S mountains
G. telescope T E L E S C O P E telescope
H. microscope M I C R O S C O P E microscope
I. night N I G H T night
J. day D A Y day

LESSON 2

PAGE 136 1. A. Read the following words three times.

A. water
B. food
C. soap
D. towels
E. medicine
F. plants
G. wet
H. dry
I. sick
J. lost

PAGE 136 1. B. Read the following. The students write the corresponding letters on the lines provided.

1. towels
2. plants
3. food and water
4. soap and medicine
5. wet and dry
6. sick, lost, and wet
7. soap, water, and towels
8. sick, medicine, and lost
9. plants, food, dry, and wet

PAGE 136 1. C. Spell each word. The students write the words on the lines provided.

A. water W A T E R water
B. food F O O D food
C. soap S O A P soap
D. towels T O W E L S towels
E. medicine M E D I C I N E medicine
F. plants P L A N T S plants
G. wet W E T wet
H. dry D R Y dry
I. sick S I C K sick
J. lost L O S T lost

LESSON 3

PAGE 140 1. A. Read the following words three times.

A. bakery
B. post office
C. hardware store
D. jewelry store
E. drugstore
F. bread
G. stamps
H. tools
I. watches

PAGE 140 1. B. Read the following. The students write the corresponding letters on the lines provided.

1. bread
2. watches
3. stamps and tools
4. post office and hardware store
5. bakery and drugstore
6. jewelry store, watches, and tools
7. bakery, bread, post office, and stamps
8. tools, hardware store, watches, and jewelry store

PAGE 140 1. C. Spell each word. The students write the words on the lines provided.

A. bakery B A K E R Y bakery
B. post office, post P O S T office O F F I C E post office
C. hardware store, hardware H A R D W A R E store S T O R E hardware store
D. jewelry store, jewelry J E W E L R Y store S T O R E jewelry store
E. drugstore D R U G S T O R E drugstore
F. bread B R E A D bread
G. stamps S T A M P S stamps
H. tools T O O L S tools
I. watches W A T C H E S watches

PAGE 142 4. A. Read the following dialog. Tell the students that there are nineteen words missing, and instruct them to put a caret (∧) wherever a word is missing.

Linda: John, stop *watching* television and listen. I'm going to drive *you* to school in *five* minutes.
John: Yes, Mother.
Linda: Do you *have* your jacket?

168   Back of the Book

John: Yes, I have *it*.
Linda: Do you have *your* books?
John: Yes, I have *them*.
Linda: John, stop watching television *and* listen.
John: *I'm* listening.
Linda: Did you *brush* your teeth?
John: Yes, I brushed *them*.
Linda: Did *you* wash your face?
John: Yes, I washed *it*.
Linda: Can you see your *sister* in the car?
John: Yes, I can see *her*.
Linda: Can you see your *father* in the car?
John: Yes, I can see *him*.
Linda: Well, then. Get your *books* and let's *go*.

Chapter 12: Summary

PAGE 144 1. A. Read the following categories three times.

A. singular nouns
B. plural nouns
C. present-tense verbs
D. past-tense verbs
E. prepositions
F. adjectives
G. singular pronouns
H. plural pronouns

PAGE 144 1. B. Read the following. The students write the corresponding letters on the lines provided.

1. adjectives
2. prepositions
3. singular pronouns
4. singular nouns and plural nouns
5. present-tense verbs and past-tense verbs
6. plural pronouns and plural nouns
7. prepositions, singular nouns, and adjectives
8. past-tense verbs, singular pronouns, and present-tense verbs

PAGE 144 1. C. Spell each word. The students write the words on the lines provided.

A. singular nouns, singular S I N G U L A R nouns N O U N S singular nouns
B. plural nouns, plural P L U R A L nouns N O U N S plural nouns
C. present-tense verbs, present P R E S E N T tense T E N S E verbs V E R B S present-tense verbs
D. past-tense verbs, past P A S T tense T E N S E verbs V E R B S past-tense verbs
E. prepositions P R E P O S I T I O N S prepositions
F. adjectives A D J E C T I V E S adjectives
G. singular pronouns, singular S I N G U L A R pronouns P R O N O U N S singular pronouns
H. plural pronouns, plural P L U R A L pronouns P R O N O U N S plural pronouns

Index

A

action verbs, 55
adjectives, 56–58, 116–119
affirmative and negative
　in past, 113
all/some/any, 58–59
alphabet, 4–5
and, or, but, 61, 63
animals, 87–89

B

be able to, 93–95
because, 94–95
before, after, between, 28–31, 35
birthday, age, 77–79

C

can, cannot, can't, 86, 88–89
cities, 10–11
city populations, 130
classroom objects, 20–23
clothing, 60–61
colors, 60–61
comes before/follows, 72–73
community places, 99–101
comparatives, 123–131
continents, 122–123
contractions and negatives with *to be*, 14–17
countries, 8–11

D

days of the week, 6–7
did, didn't, 106–107
direction words, 52–54
do and *does* with *have*, 39–40, 42–43
do not, does not, 40, 42–43

E

-er adjectives with *than*, 125–126

F

family terms, 36–40, 44, 46–51
future with *will*, 69–72, 76–79

G

games, 90
get, 141
going-to future 65–66

H

had, 103
have, 36–39
holidays, 75

I

is there?, are there?, 6–7
it is, they are, 11

K

know how to, 91

L

larger, smaller, 123

M

measurement terms, 126, 128
money, 127
months of the year, 72–77
more/fewer than, 130–131
more/less than, 128–129
musical instruments, 90

N

names, 6–7
nationalities, 13–15
numbers **10-100**, 29–31
　1-10, 2–3
　10-20, 29–31
　above **100**, 120–121

O

object pronouns, 132–133, 135, 139, 141–142
objects, 132–133, 135, 137–139, 141–142
oceans, 122–123
opposites, 117–119
ordinal numbers, 74-76

P

parts of the body, 41–43, 84–86
parts of the head, 24–25, 85
possessive adjectives, 24–25, 45–47
prepositions of place, 20–23, 25–31, 34–35
present continuous, 61–63
present tenses, 53–59, 61–66

Q

questions with *to be*, 13–19

S

seasons, 116, 118
shapes, 96
short answers with *to be*, 16–19
simple past, 108, 110–111, 113, 115
simple present, 53–54, 57–59
singular/plural, 10–11
sports, 64–65
　equipment, 92–95
stores, 140–141
subject pronouns with *to be*, 12–15

T

telephone numbers, 3
the same as, 127
there is, there are, 6–7
times, 68–71
to be, 6–7, 10–11, 13–19
to have, 36–40, 42–43, 45, 47–50

W

was, were, wasn't, 97–98, 100–101
weather adjectives, 114–115
weather words, 114–115
what is?, what are?, 28–30
where is?, where are?, 34–35
who is?, 26–27, 48
who is?, who are?, 48
will not, won't, 76–79
will, 69–71

Z

zero, 2–3

170　Index